Flying Boats

Flying Boats

My Father's War in the Mediterranean

Alex Frame

Victoria University Press

VICTORIA UNIVERSITY PRESS
Victoria University of Wellington
PO Box 600 Wellington
vuw.ac.nz/vup

Copyright © Alex Frame 2007
First published 2007

ISBN 978-0-86473-562-1

National Library of New Zealand Cataloguing-in-Publication Data
Frame, Alex, 1946–
Flying boats : my father's war in the Mediterranean / Alex Frame.
Includes bibliographical references and index.
ISBN 978-0-86473-562-1
1. Frame, Alec, 1916–1983. 2. Air pilots, Military—New Zealand
—Biography. 3. World War, 1939–1945—Aerial operations,
New Zealand. 4. World War, 1939–1945—Mediterranean Region.
5. Sunderland (Seaplanes).
I. Title.940.544993—dc 22

Printed by Astra Print, Wellington

Contents

For the grandchildren,

so that they might know something
of the times and deeds of their great-grandfather
and precursor, the flying boat pilot.

1. Introduction

The roots of this story are the flight logbooks of my father, who lived between 1916 and 1983, and was a flying-boat pilot in war and afterwards in peace. The three logbooks span a career of 30 years. The first, now held in the Royal New Zealand Air Force Museum at Wigram, near Christchurch, covers the period of earliest flying in 1938, through World War II, and on to 1950. The second, from 1950 to 1960, records flying in Sydney and then Tahiti, and the third, more flying in Tahiti and Fiji from 1960 to a final flight in 1969. These two logbooks are in my possession.

Twenty years after my father's death, I found myself turning to these carefully kept records of his life as a flying-boat pilot. They record a total of 7500 hours of flight, almost all as captain of aircraft. They list the date of every flight made, the type and registration sign of the aircraft, the names of senior flight crew and sometimes of particularly distinguished passengers, the places of departure and arrival, and the duration of each flight with a day/night allocation, along with notes about mechanical failures, abnormal weather, or incidents during the flight. In the war period, the purpose of the mission is also noted. 'Alec', as my father was known to my mother and his contemporaries, made his entries as carefully as he flew: the logbooks are well kept, written with a laconic style in his crisp and distinctive printing.

Beyond the information it preserves, the logbook has a quality of its own. It has been physically with the pilot during the events and journeys recorded: a final taskmaster for the tired flyer, the elated flyer, and the frightened flyer. Built to withstand the battering and abrasion of constant handling, of packing and unpacking, it has endured the flight decks and hotel rooms, the sea spray and sand storm, the humidity and chemicals. Oil, metal, salt, sand, cigarette smoke, liquor, sweat, and gasoline are all sponged up and preserved in its canvas cladding and yellowing pages. The log exudes these smells, and with them a kind of secret knowledge and excitement.

YEAR 1941		AIRCRAFT		PILOT, OR 1ST PILOT	2ND PILOT, PUPIL OR PASSENGER	DUTY (INCLUDING RESULTS AND REMA
MONTH	DATE	Type	No.			
—	—	—	—	—	—	— TOTALS BROUGHT FORW
APRIL						
	1	SUNDERLAND	T9046	SELF, F/LT. LAMOND, SGT. MASSAM		PATROL W.A.A. - SIGHTED ITAL HOSPITAL SHIP.
	3		T9046	SELF,	"	PATROL W.A.A. - SIGHTED ITALIAN HOSPITAL SHIP.
	4		T9046	"	"	"	SCARAMANGA - ALEX
	10		T9046	"	P/O PARÉ	SGT. MASSAM	ALEX. - CAIRO.
	11		T9046	"	"	"	CAIRO - SCARAMANGA
					A.C.M. SIR.A. LONGMORE. A.O.C. i.c. ME GEN. SIR.A. WAVELL G.O.C. + 15 PASS.	SCARAMANGA - CAIRO.
	13		T9046	"	"		
	13		T9046	"	P/O PARÉ, SGT. MASSAM	CAIRO - ABOUKIR

Figure 1: Some entries for early April 1941, from the wartime logbook.

The logbooks are therefore both authoritative records and mystical objects. As records they tell us with precision and accuracy where pilots and passengers were at particular times, what they were doing, and in what aircraft. A major function of the logbook is to keep an accurate tally of the hours flown by the pilot: hours in command and hours of night-flying are carefully listed and certified periodically by authorised officials. The log is a highly reliable source which, as a contemporaneous and audited record, is almost always to be trusted above other sources as to the details set out.

Yet, if these sparse entries were to be brought to life more than 60 years later, much supportive explanation and background would be needed: the qualities and capacities of the flying boats and their pilots, the state of the war at the time and the roles and motives of some major military and political figures, the geography and climate of the war theatre, the perceptions of the participants and their personal histories, and the surviving photographic record. These matters could not be illuminated without reference to my father's family background, schooling, and training as an airman, and to technical aspects of the design and development of the flying boats concerned. I soon discovered surviving comrades who had flown with my father in the events described and resolved to interview them.

The role of the Sunderland flying-boat squadrons – and in particular of Alec's Sunderland T9046 – in the Allied withdrawals from Greece and Crete in the spring of 1941 soon loomed as the natural centrepiece of the account. Not only did this period make the most demands on machines and pilots, but it also provided the richest strategic context, calling for consideration of the control and direction of British war policy in the Middle East and the controversies surrounding the British War Cabinet's decision to send forces to Greece in 1941.

Historical reconstruction has a 'compression' effect (if I may borrow a term from computer language). Just as the 'pixels' of a digital image are reduced to the minimum capable of interpretation by the viewer's imagination, so is the storyteller forced by the limitations of available record and surviving memory to rely on a few salient features combined with the reader's imaginative powers. There is the further aspect that the reconstructor of events knows the subsequent story: how things worked out after the events reconstructed, and how the events have come to be viewed by posterity. This knowledge was not available to the recorder of the day, and the sensation experienced by the later reader may be akin to that of the 'dramatic irony' enjoyed by a theatre audience, to whom the dramatist allows information not vouchsafed to the characters, so granting it an illusion of omniscient wisdom.

Figure 2: This picture was taken on 31 July 1940 at Oban, on the west coast of Scotland, by RAF photographer Stanley Devon. The Hutcheson Memorial Needle on Kerrera is just visible on the extreme left. My father, on the right, has under his arm the logbook on which this account is based, and is about to exercise the service captain's privilege of last-boarding his Mark I Sunderland. The other airman is another New Zealander, T.P. Gibson (later Wing Commander and DFC).

One of the sources of our interest in viewing historic film footage, for example of British Prime Minister Neville Chamberlain descending from his aeroplane declaring 'peace in our time', is our knowledge of the subsequent events which in that case rendered the declaration tragically false. When we view the relics of Scott's expedition to Antarctica, we know that Scott and his companions will lose their lives in generally heroic circumstances. This knowledge amplifies the 'charge' carried by a simple diary entry or an item of equipment associated with the events.

Photographs and other images can be a point of entry into historical reconstruction as well. The work of Max Sebald exploits the sometimes electric connections between picture and word which can result:

> ... his own writerly resurrection of photographs and paintings ... aimed always at the detail which revives the life that the still image has frozen. He holds on to the traces the skaters have left behind in the ice in the late afternoon ... [1]

Some of the images in this book are from our family albums, others from the Imperial War Museum in London and other historical collections, and others again were taken on my travels to research this account.

Place, too, can be an important element of historical re-presentation. Although I am sure it is more widespread, close contact with Polynesian culture in childhood has left me with a sense of the pregnancy of place – the first identity to be greeted in Polynesian ritual, before the ancestors and the living. The features of the land and sea, the smells and light effects, the climatic conditions and moods, are links to the experience of our forebears and to their deeds. A rusted iron mooring-ring embedded in long-forgotten concrete at Alness, still exposed to the corrosive winter of the waters of Cromarty Firth in northern Scotland, can tell the visitor 60 years later something about conditions there in 1942, when Sunderland crews trained uncomfortably and hazardously to join the desperate battle being fought out between U-boats and convoys in the grey waters of the Atlantic. I have not hesitated to describe my visits in 2003 and 2005 to the places in New Zealand, the British Isles and the Mediterranean which featured in my father's education and training, and later in military action. One strand of the account is accordingly the story of my investigation itself.

This method of reconstruction, reliant on direct contact with word, object, image, and place, may be the nearest we can get to the 'time-machine' of fable and cinema. Across the distance of time it is the only way to ask, as Homer has King Alcinous inquire of Odysseus in a much earlier Mediterranean adventure:

> Come on then, answer me, tell me the truth now:
> Where have you wandered? What were the places you went to?
> Which men were there, what cities or people who lived well?
> Tell us of both – the wilder sort, the cruel and unfair,
> And those who were mindful of Gods and kindly with strangers.[2]

Alec's war logbook contains a page listing 'Places visited by Flying Boat' during the course of the war. The list broadly reflects the three phases of Alec's war: 'home waters', the Mediterranean, and West Africa.

> United Kingdom: Calshot. Pembroke Dock. Mount Batten. Falmouth. Rochester (Short Bros.). Woodhaven. Oban. Holyhead. Invergordon. Sullom Voe (Shetlands). Castletown (Hebrides). Bowmore. Stranraer. Helensburgh. Loch Erne (Northern Ireland). Tobermory. Gourock. Largs. Loch Ness (Caledonian Canal).

> France: Brest; Gibraltar; Malta: Kalafrana, St. Paul's Bay; Tunisia: Gulf of Hammamet; Egypt: Alexandria Harbour, Aboukir, Cairo; Crete: Suda Bay, Sphakia; Greece: Scaramanga, Nauplia (Argos Bay); Palestine: Sea of Galilee; Iraq: Basra (Shatt al Arab); Anglo-Egyptian Sudan: Khartoum (Gordon's Tree); Uganda: Kampala (Port Bell); French Equatorial Africa: Stanleyville, Pointe Noire; Belgian Congo: Leopoldville; Nigeria: Lagos; Sierra Leone: Freetown, Jui; Gambia: Bathurst (Half Die); Senegal: Dakar; Mauretania: Port Etienne; Canada: Boucherville, Lac des Neiges; Newfoundland: Gander Lake; Bermuda; United States: Elizabeth City; Liberia: Fisherman's Lake; Ivory Coast: Abijan.

I should anticipate a natural question: why is little detail given here about events after Alec's cross-Africa flight in July 1941? There are two answers. First, there are no links to the broad course and direction of the war comparable with those I discovered in respect of the Middle East period in 1941. In the absence of these the logbook by itself produces only a long succession of patrols and

training flights without discernible context. Second, full coverage
of the entire war period would require several further chapters: one
on the crushing boredom of station life in West Africa, another on
the difficult and surprisingly dangerous time Alec spent training
flying-boat crews in northern Scotland, yet another on his second
stint at Alexandria in 1942. And that's just the war period. Full
treatment of my father's flying career would also call for a chapter
on his post-war civil flying, one on Sydney operations in 1950, and
finally a more complete treatment of Tahiti operations, which are
only skimmed here. Even the most loyal reader might be overdosing
on flying boats by then!

What I have tried to do instead is give the reader a sketch of
this bigger picture, along with some flashes of detail, but to zoom
in on the period of his command of Sunderland T9046, from
December 1940 to June 1941. This period, because of its nature
and its intersection with wider political and military events, can be
linked to what I have judged to be interesting themes. My father,
who might not have approved of this whole enterprise, would have
been somewhat reassured to learn that the 'star' of this book – if it
has one – is really Sunderland T9046.

2. Other Drums

When a boy growing up in Tahiti, to which Pacific island my father's profession of flying-boat captain had led our family by 1953, I was taken into the control cabins of the Sandringham 'Bermuda' flying-boat F-OBIP[3] ('Bravo India Papa' was the call-sign we heard crackling over the radio) and Catalina F-OAYD[4] ('Yankee Delta'). I sat entranced in the co-pilot's seat on several flights between Tahiti and Bora Bora, while on another occasion we flew in the Bermuda to Rangiroa in the Tuamotus. It was of course a great thrill and, needless to say, my boyhood ambition was to become a pilot of one of these magnificent aircraft. My father discouraged this aspiration, warning of a new age of flying in which the pilot's basic functions would increasingly be taken over by machines. Today we learn that the aircraft of the future, especially military types, may dispense entirely with pilots, being called UAVs or 'unmanned aerial vehicles'. A modern aviation joke is that these future aircraft will carry a pilot and a dog: the pilot to watch the automatic controls and the dog to bite the pilot if he threatens to touch anything.

I grew up with flying boats, in the way that farming families grow up with tractors. The sound of Pratt and Whitney aero-engines, which powered both the Bermuda and the Catalinas of the French company RAI (Réseau Aérien Interinsulaire), was full of reassurance. As a 10-year-old I would hear the approaching drone and overhead roar of these engines through the open verandah of my classroom, or with Tahitian and Chinese friends fishing near Pomare's Tomb with the Benedictine bottle on top, or with my mother, Penny, at Arue in the cluster of *niau*-roofed huts which was our home. It meant that Papa Alec was back, and safe, and would soon be with us again. All was well in the isolated but happy universe that was pre-aerodrome Tahiti in the 1950s.

The same sound, climbing to full take-off power, could sometimes be heard at dawn, as a flying boat got under way on a 'mercy flight' to search for an overdue fisherman in Raiatea, or to bring an acute medical case from the Tuamotus to Papeete for treatment. The telephone would have rung in the night and, awoken, we children would find our father alert over charts on the dining table, plotting courses and calculating fuel loads. The khaki shorts and open-necked tunic and two brown leather flying-cases (one of which I later inherited for university) would be readied and 'le capitaine Frame' driving into the cool *tiare*-scented air of the early dawn, through the coconut plantations and banana groves towards the base at Fa'aa.

Figure 3: The 'Bermuda' class Short Sandringham F-OBIP in RAI livery undergoing maintenance at Fa'aa base, Tahiti, around 1959. This aircraft, restored to this livery, is now in the French Air Museum at Le Bourget, near Paris.

At Collège Paul Gauguin in Papeete, I read in French Saint-Exupéry's exciting and emotional accounts of pioneering airmail flights across the Atlantic and in South America in the 1930s. That pilot, later mysteriously missing on a 1944 wartime mission, addressed his lost comrade:

> Even though, Guillaumet, your days and nights are spent operating pressure gauges, balancing over gyroscopes, your stethoscope on the engines, wrestling with fifteen tons of metal: your problems are in the end the problems of human beings, and you share this noble focus with mountaineers. Like the poet, you can taste the early dawn. From the dark

depths of hard nights you have yearned for that pale bloom, that light welling out of the eastern darklands. Such a miraculous melting fountain has sometimes healed you when you thought to die.[5]

Inevitably, W.E. Johns's *Biggles* books were part of my early reading in English. Another book that stands out in memory is the gripping account by James Norman Hall – better known for his *Mutiny on the Bounty* – of the American Lafayette Squadron's flying in France in World War I. I came across this work at the Hall family house in Arue, which our family frequently visited in the 1950s, having become friends with Jimmy's widow, Lala, his beautiful daughter, Nancy, and her convivial husband, Nick Rutgers. The children of our two households were often thrown together by social occasions.

In the late 1950s, when my sisters and I had been sent to school in New Zealand, we travelled back to Tahiti for school holidays on TEAL's 'Coral Route'– the delightful three-day service which took passengers by Solent flying boat (another civil variant of the wartime Sunderland) from Auckland to Fiji, with a stay at the now sadly derelict Grand Pacific Hotel, on to Samoa and Aggie Grey's hotel, and on the third day, after a lunch stop at Aitutaki in the Cook Islands, to Papeete harbour at sunset. A number of the TEAL captains had been wartime comrades of my father, among them the legendary Joe Shephard, and Mauri McGreal, who in recent years has written a vivid and instructive account of his flying career.[6] Both had been with Alec, by then an old hand, in the cold of Alness, near Invergordon in north-east Scotland, when the New Zealand 490 Squadron was formed and trained on Catalinas in 1943.

When non-flying days coincided with school holidays, I would sometimes accompany my father by car – in early days a World War II jeep painted white, later a hump-backed grey Austin A30 – to the flying-boat base on the island at Fa'aa, connected to the mainland by a causeway. There were often repair and maintenance matters to be discussed with the French and Tahitian ground staff. Keeping flying boats serviceable is a tricky business at the best of times, but more so when beset by tropical climate and geographical isolation from spare parts. The heady smell of aero engines, anti-corrosion products, and aviation gasoline, and the friendly relations with the crew and staff, remain as warm memories. At a company Christmas party, Alec once donned a full Father Christmas suit with white beard and ran up the engines of a Catalina on the tarmac, to emerge from the rear door with a bag of presents for a wide-eyed gathering of us company children.

Another famous name pops up in the Tahiti logbooks: American aviator Clyde Pangborn (1894–1958), nicknamed 'Upside Down' Pangborn for his propensity for slow-rolling aircraft onto their backs in his barnstorming days in the 1920s. Pangborn was principally known for making the first non-stop flight across the Pacific. In October 1931, in his Bellanca Skyrocket, powered by a single 425-horsepower Pratt and Whitney engine, Pangborn flew from Misawa in Japan to Wenatchee in Washington state – a distance of 4558 miles on a flight lasting a mind-numbing 41 hours. In March 1957, after waiting for nearly a month in San Francisco for favourable winds, Pangborn and Alec together flew Catalina F-OAYD (pictured below) on its delivery flight from Alameda to Honolulu (16 hours), on to Canton Island (14 hours), and then to Tahiti (another 12 hours). The details of these flights are set out in my father's second logbook.

Figure 4: RAI's Catalina F-OAYD moored at Borabora, about 1959.

In September 1956, RAI had sent Alec to New Orleans to select, recondition, and bring back a World War II Catalina for use on the air routes around Tahiti. Weeks stretched into months as delay followed delay. It took nearly six months for test flights to begin in February 1957. Life at 'Frame Village' settled down to a fatherless routine. One night my mother had an intruder in her bedroom – he was driven out when Penny fought furiously. Next day the British Consul, Freddie Devenish, a family friend of Falstaffian proportions, came out to Arue and, followed by a gaggle of curious bystanders and mimicking children, walked the perimeter of our garden brandishing a very large revolver, finally discharging it noisily at an old tree stump in an unconvincing assertion of the retributory capacity of Her Britannic Majesty's authority, before all retired for lunch and drinks.

Figure 5: Growing up with flying boats. The author (bottom of ladder) with sisters Margaret (top) and Susan in Tahiti about 1958, with Bermuda in RAI livery as backdrop.

Eventually, the Catalina was airworthy in America and set off for the South Pacific. I remember its arrival in Tahiti. I was eleven years old and had not seen my father for six months. My mother and my sisters and I were waiting excitedly at Fa'aa base with a small crowd of officials and friends. We first heard, then saw, the Catalina grow from a dot in the sky to a gleaming, roaring, banking, silver flying boat. It turned into its approach and slid out of view beneath the coconut trees hiding the alighting area of the lagoon. Then . . . silence. The crowd looked in vain towards the headland around which the aircraft must appear. After some minutes, there it was at last – the taxiing Catalina, which soon moored close to the jetty and cut engines. The rear hatch opened and I caught sight of a chaotic cabin with gear strewn about, very unlike my father's tidy habit. Two unshaven and bleary-eyed airmen (the venerable Pangborn and my father) emerged, climbed into the tender at separate ends, and, on reaching the jetty, strode off wordlessly in different directions. It was plain that something was wrong.

Although the incident was quickly forgotten in the excitement of recovering our father – and of exploring the wonderful array of hi-fi equipment and new long-playing record albums of exciting music, including Elvis Presley, which Alec had brought back with him – I have in retrospect connected one or two remarks with my memory of that arrival. I now think that the Pangborn/Frame landing of Catalina F-OAYD in Tahiti on 22 March 1957, after the long flight from Canton Island, had somehow gone wrong, nearly led to disaster, and been the subject of recrimination between the pilots, the details of which could only be guessed at.

Flying-boat operations in the central Pacific in the 1950s were basic. Radar and even radio direction-finding systems were non-existent. Navigation across the great ocean expanses between small islands and low atolls left little margin for error. The primary method was 'dead reckoning', involving use of a sextant from the flying boat's astrodome to take sights of the sun or stars, plotting courses with ruler and pencil, and judging drift by observation of the sea surface in daylight. Changing weather conditions had to be anticipated and reacted to. Saint-Exupéry again, writing of his fellow pilots opening the transatlantic mail routes in the early 1930s:

> One needs a tool to enter into contact with the world. One needs a carpenter's plane or a plough. The peasant, in ploughing bit by bit, discovers the secrets of the earth . . . Thus did these men, through their cockpit controls, through the magic of their instruments of work, acquire a kind of peasant wisdom. They too met those elementary divinities – night, day, mountain, sea and storm . . . They watched their skies, quite simply, as those earthlings would have watched their vines. It was the source of their serenity.[7]

The flavour of those Tahiti years, and of island flying operations in the 1950s, as well as my father's wry sense of humour and accurate expression, are all present in an unpublished short story titled 'Other Drums', written in retirement 20 years later, when he worked in a plastics factory in Auckland during the week and travelled at weekends with Penny to what became their retirement home at Cook's Beach in the Coromandel. It recounts an island-hopping journey in the Tuamotu and Gambier groups with French officials in Air Tahiti's Grumman Mallard F-OAII in June 1953.

Readers may become curious, as this account proceeds, to hear my father's own voice and manner of speaking about flying-boat operations. This story is to my knowledge the only source capable of satisfying that reasonable curiosity, and I have reproduced it without alteration, but with the addition of two of Alec's navigational maps made for the expedition, from the originals in my possession. The crew were flight engineers Maurice Diard and Jean Bataille, the former subsequently killed in the crash of Catalina F–OAVV in Raiatea on 19 February 1958, when the right wing-tip float hit the water during a shallow turn for the final approach in dangerous 'flat calm' conditions. Captain R.C. Allais and crew and 12 of the 23 passengers lost their lives in the accident, which occurred when my father was on leave in New Zealand, installing my sisters and me in boarding schools.

Of the 1953 journey in the elegant twin-engined Grumman Mallard, my father wrote:

OTHER DRUMS

I thought, when I left the air and the sea and the islands, that I would be finished with drums – those ubiquitous fuel containers, channel markers, work stands, water tanks, mooring buoys and mosquitoe breeders. But no. Here they are on the land too, marking the path to follow when roads are under repair.

On the way to my work in a plastics factory I drive between them every day. I wonder if we shall ever have plastic drums? But I must keep off that subject. My wife warns me that plastics are beginning to dominate my thinking.

I shall go back to the drums. Metal drums. Markers are what drums mostly are.

There was that day of the drums at Niau. Quite a day that was . . .

I put the Grumman Mallard into a fairly steep left hand turn around the central lagoon on the atoll at 1000 feet. I was looking for a clear coral free alighting path, a mooring for the aircraft, and a boat of some kind, or even canoes, to transport my passengers and crew ashore.

The lagoon appeared to be of even depth with no obstructions. A petrol drum was anchored 20 yards from what appeared to be a soft muddy shore near a T-shaped jetty. So the mooring was there. But where?, oh where? was the means of transportation ashore.

I circled again, thinking perhaps I had missed a boat coming along the edge of the lagoon. Nothing. The reception committee was clearly visible on the jetty. But of marine craft there was no sign. It began to look as though we would all be swimming ashore.

So our luck had finally run out, and the organisation had broken down on the second to last day of our six day visit to eleven different atolls in that time.

A month before we had completed the planning of this expedition. Drums of aviation gasoline were sent to certain points on our proposed route by island schooner and we had to assume that they would arrive intact and be stored safely until our arrival.

The crew of our Grumman Mallard amphibian aircraft consisted of myself as Pilot and Navigator and two French Flight Engineers. One more engineer than usual in case of

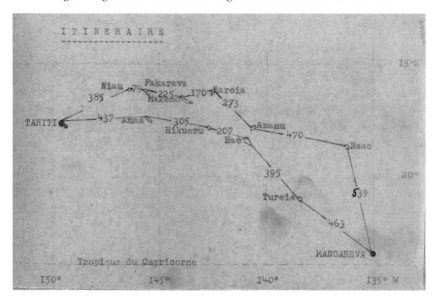

Figure 6: Alec's map of the Grumman Mallard's Tuamotu itinerary in 1953.

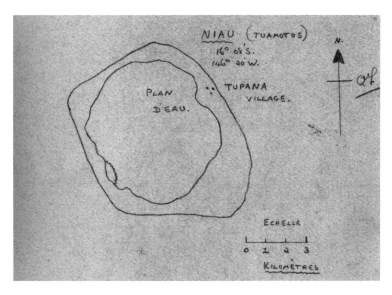

Figure 7: Alec's signed map of Niau made in 1953.

breakdown "out in the blue". Our passengers were four French Chiefs of Service – Public Works, Health, Education and Agriculture, who were normally based in Tahiti, one of our own Company Representatives, and one interpreter for the French/Tahitian translation tasks. Nine in all on board.

A week before our departure Radio Tahiti broadcast on three consecutive days instructions in both the French and Tahitian languages about our itinerary with dates, times of arrival, numbers of beds and meals required, and facilities to be provided for the aircraft which would always use the sheltered central lagoon and not the open sea.

A mooring was to be prepared at the eleven places to be visited and boats provided to ferry passengers and crew ashore. Many of the atolls had never been visited by an aircraft before so that instructions had to be really detailed and comprehensive.

Our schedule was a fairly tight one – generally a morning flight to one atoll where we stayed for lunch, then an afternoon flight to another where we would night stop. Everywhere, of course, we had been royally received – a colour hoisting, to the accompaniment of the Marseillaise sung by the shrill voices of the school children all dressed up in their Sunday best – decorated archways, fences and buildings, all done with that versatile coconut palm frond. Then a native feast interspersed with oratory from both sides and generally native drumming and dancing.

Flies being a problem in all these atolls we even had teams of girls standing behind us flapping gaily coloured pareu cloths to chase away these pests. We were always greeted on arrival with a necklace of sea shells or flowers, presented by a young girl who added a kiss on both cheeks to complete the ceremony.

For the feast one was not properly dressed without a couronne, or crown, on the head. This was ingeniously contrived of plaited coconut fronds interlaced with the lovely colourful local flowers such as hibiscus or the white Tiare Tahiti with its exotic lingering perfume.

For four days all had gone as planned. No mechanical faults with the aircraft and all facilities had been provided as requested in our broadcast radio message.

Figure 8: Grumman Mallard F-OAII at Taiohae, Nuku Hiva, in the Marquesas Islands in October 1953. The Air Tahiti amphibian had just made the first flight from Tahiti to Nuku Hiva and afterwards bore on its nose the name bestowed there: 'Te Manunui o Nuku Hiva' (the Big Bird of Nuku Hiva).

We had visited Anaa, Hikueru, Hao, Tureia (near Mururoa, the French atomic testing atoll), Mangareva in the Gambier Islands, Reao, Amanu, Raroia (the Kon Tiki island), Makemo, Fakarava, and here we were over Niau, our last atoll before our return to Papeete the next day. And here was where we were going to be in a mess. Why? oh Why? no boats.

I put the aircraft down and taxied to the mooring and stopped the engines. I sat for a moment wondering how best to explain to the passengers our predicament about getting ashore. Apologetic French phrases were forming themselves in my mind when suddenly I noticed that the jetty near where we were moored had altered shape. The head of the T-shape had detached itself from the body and was approaching the aircraft. On this platform, floating on empty drums, was a reception committee of four high officials. It was gaily decorated and its method of propulsion? . . . Twelve stalwart natives in pareu loin cloths were swimming it towards us. They manoeuvred it expertly alongside the rear door of the aircraft and my passengers began to disembark followed by the crew and lastly myself.

Perhaps they had not bargained for such a big pilot but my 215 pounds must have been the last straw. As the swimmers set off once more to propel our floating platform back towards the jetty and terra firma the floor became gradually awash and then submerged slightly, just enough for the water to lap over the tops of our shoes.

We all continued to look as though it was the happiest day of our lives to be with the residents of Niau.

And I shall never forget the sound of thirteen pairs of shoes, full of wet socks and water, squelching down that jetty to the reception ceremonies awaiting us on dry land.

Just a small miscalculation on the buoyancy problem but full marks for ingenuity. Don't you agree?

To be quite honest with you, one pair of the thirteen pairs of shoes making such succulent noises along that jetty was also making a sloshing noise. The reason being that there were no socks inside to absorb the water and cushion the effect. So this small deficiency in my wardrobe became apparent to everyone present.

And speaking of socks, believe it or not, DRUMBEAT is the name of a new brown shade of nylon stockings for

women. When my wife showed me a card with the words
KANT RUN DRUMBEAT printed on it I knew that she
expected me to wonder aloud when we would be wearing
plastic socks.

But I didn't say anything of the sort because my mind was
away on those drums of yesteryear – those drums that could
neither run nor beat – just those drums neath rustling palms,
leaking fuel on to the white coral sands, or bobbing in crystal
clear blue lagoons to mark the dark brown tentacles of living
coral heads reaching for the fragile hull of a magnificent
flying machine . . .

On his first retirement from flying, in 1963, my father brought
the family base back to New Zealand. After some struggles with a
grocery business in Auckland, for which I made van deliveries in my
early university years, in 1967 he and Penny moved to Fiji, where
he flew for Air Pacific until suffering a back injury in a fall from the
wing of another Grumman Mallard[8] while carrying out a ground
inspection in April 1969. This injury led to his final retirement from
flying. His last flight was – flying boats to the end – in Air Pacific's
Mallard F-BC from Nadi to Vunisea and back on 29 August 1969.
My parents eventually settled into retirement, first at Cook's Beach
and later at Sumner in Christchurch, where Alec died suddenly of
heart failure at the age of 67 in 1983. It was out of the blue – he had
caught a trout in the Waimakariri River the day before.

Alec talked almost never about the war. On the rare occasions
when he did, it was to create a general impression of having had an
uneventful and tedious time away from the danger and excitement
of the single-seat fighter combat in Spitfires and Hurricanes featured
in *Boys' Own* magazines. It was only later, when I had resort to
historical works on the role played by flying boats in the war, and in
particular in the Mediterranean, and began to study his logbooks,
that I came to realise that Alec's war had its full measure of danger,
death, and disaster. Keith Ovenden makes an insightful observation
in his life of Dan Davin:

This, surely, was the true terror of war, and it could only be
broached as a topic of domestic conversation, if at all, by
reformulation into something else. From this sprang the habit
of camouflaging ugly truths that, even if expressed, were

otherwise unlikely to be understood. Nevertheless, and behind
the camouflage, such incidents remained the hard material of
which the experience of the war was composed, and their
presence, whether distorted in the recollection, or suppressed
into tormented silence, was corrosive. They ate away at a
soldier's sense of moral connection with others, promoting a
degree of alienation that is easy to underestimate.[9]

Alec's wartime comrade, Henry Lamond, of whom more later in
this account, told me that my father developed hearing loss in his
left ear as a result of exposure to the sound blast of Pegasus engines
through the Mark I Sunderland cockpit window which he would
often open for better visibility while taxiing and manoeuvring.
Henry thought that, at the end of the war, BOAC had turned Alec
down as a prospective captain for this reason. Many old Sunderland
hands went to the British civilian flying boats after the war, and
thence to the big jets in the 1960s. Had this happened, Alec would
not have ended up in Tahiti, and the history of our family would
have been very different – not least, the connection with the South
Pacific and New Zealand might not have been resumed.

Figure 9: Alec at the controls of a Trans Oceanic Airways flying boat at Rose Bay,
Sydney, 1952.

3. Oamaru Origins

MY cousin Janet Frame was a wonderful writer with a world-wide reputation whose death in 2004 was an occasion for national mourning. I read her first book, *Owls Do Cry*, as a 13-year-old schoolboy and was swept away by its evocative power and artistry. She made words exciting, powerful, and gave to the profession of writer an almost religious mystique. In the first volume of her autobiography Janet provided some details of the origins and ancestry of our family and of life in Oamaru in the 1930s. Of the family's earliest origins, she wrote:

> As a child I used to boast that the Frames 'came over with William of Orange'. I have since learned that this may have been so, for Frame is a version of Fleming, Flamand, from the Flemish weavers who settled in the lowlands of Scotland in the fourteenth century.[10]

Janet and my father shared a grandfather, inevitably another Alex Frame, born in 1855 in Hamilton, Scotland – a stoker and blacksmith. And a grandmother, Grandma Frame, born Mary Paterson in Paisley, Scotland, in 1857, who began working in a cotton mill when she was eight years old, came to New Zealand in her teens, and signed her marriage papers with a cross. Janet wrote:

> I remember her first as a tall woman in a long, black dress . . . Her skin was dark, her black hair frizzy, and although she talked in Scottish, the songs she sang were of the American Deep South . . . 'Carry me back to ole Virginny'.[11]

The records of 'assisted immigrants' in Archives New Zealand in Wellington reveal that a 'single woman', Mary Paterson, an 18-year-old domestic servant from Edinburgh, sailed from Glasgow on 7 May 1874 to arrive in Dunedin on 25 July 1874.[12] The ship was the *Mairi Bhan* – Gaelic for 'Fair Mary'. Immigrants would no doubt in later life talk around the family fireside of their shipboard experiences, and children and grandchildren would have collected many impressions from such stories.

The marriage of Alex and Mary took place on 11 May 1877 at the house of Mr Robert Fulton in Coquet Street, Oamaru, with the groom's occupation given as 'stoker'. Janet Frame listed the twelve children of that marriage, and I have emphasised in her text the names of the brothers who were respectively Alec's and her fathers:

> . . . none remains now of that Frame family of eight sons
> – John, **Alex**, Thomas, Robert, William Francis, Walter
> Henry, **George Samuel**, Charles Allan – and four daughters –
> Margaret, Mary, Isabella Woods. The fourth, my namesake,
> died at thirteen months . . . [13]

The brothers 'spent their lives with engines and movement', wrote Janet. My grandfather, Alex, born in 1880, became a taxi-driver – the first in Oamaru with his big Chrysler – and Janet's father, George, a railwayman. Alex married Jemima Bain in 1907 and made a home in Oamaru, where my father was born in 1916, the youngest of three children, with two older sisters, Jess and May. In the early 1930s George brought his family, including the 6-year-old writer-to-be, to Oamaru in the course of his work for the Railways. Janet relates:

> Our first night in Oamaru, we stayed with Aunty Mima
> (whom we thought of as Aunty *Miner*) and Uncle Alex, the
> taxi driver, on Wharfe Street on the South Hill, and the
> next morning we went to where we were to live for the next
> fourteen years: Fifty-six Eden Street, Oamaru.[14]

Later in the 1930s, Grandad Frame died in his sleep: 'he was put in a coffin in the front room with the blinds pulled down so that everyone in the street knew that someone in the house had died; that was the custom . . . '[15] Janet describes the funeral and 'the uncles with their shy Frame look and the particular set of the lips that said, "Everything should be perfect. Why isn't it?" And on Sunday . . . we all went to the cemetery on the South Hill to put flowers on Grandad's grave . . . '[16]

My father's sister May was a favourite auntie. After we started boarding school in New Zealand, my sisters and I would sometimes stay on Uncle Tom and Auntie May's dairy farm at Mangapai up in the far north of New Zealand during school holidays if we did not go home, as Tahiti still was. In 1963 my cousin Tim Williamson and I visited Oamaru, worked for a few weeks in the Pukeuri freezing works, and discovered the vacant section in Wharfe Street where our parents' childhood home had just been demolished. In 1996, towards the end of her life, Auntie May wrote this about growing up in Oamaru in the 1920s and 30s:

> Looking back I realise it was a hell of a place to grow up! There was the South Hill and the North End. And there was prohibition. South School Skites, we used to say & North School Rats! We lived in a big house on the South Hill & our poor relations lived down on the flats in a small house, & the only time we went down, there seemed to be a death in their family.[17]

In June 2004 I travelled to Oamaru in search of my father's childhood, installing myself in the Queens Hotel, an old-style stone building erected in 1880. Across the street, the archivists at the North Otago Museum were helpful: they guided me to some photographs of my great-grandfather – 'Stoker Alex' we might call him – wielding a pick on the Oamaru railway line, and of my grandfather – 'Taxi Alex', to continue the method of distinguishing the many Alexanders – alongside his big Chrysler in the 1920s and 30s. An obituary in the

Figure 10: The author by the grave of 'Taxi Alex' at South Hill cemetery, Oamaru, June 2004.

Figure 11: Oamaru Railway Station, opened in 1900, at sunrise in June 2004 – much as it would have been when Alec left it in 1935.

Oamaru Mail recorded my grandfather's death in 1941. It called him 'a very well-known resident' and mentioned his birth in Oamaru, saying that 'his parents were pioneers of North Otago, his father having come to New Zealand as shipmate of Mr H. Pheloung'.[18] The archivists gave me a map of the Oamaru cemetery on South Hill marked with the rough position of Taxi Alex's grave. 'There's just "FRAME" on it,' they said as I left.

Later, up on South Hill, I did a grid-search in the marked area and at length found an overgrown double plot with no headstone and the promised single word 'FRAME' just discernible on a heavily encrusted white stone plaque embedded in concrete. Here Taxi Alex went down on 28 June 1941, near the corner of Greta and Test streets, attended no doubt by the usual family mourners. But his son 'Lex', as the family called my father, was far away – with Sunderland T9046 on Lake Victoria in Uganda. As the winter sun dropped and a storm brewed from the glowering south, I did some basic maintenance on the grave with tools from my rental car, scraping at the plaque until it recovered the pale glow of Oamaru stone.

Unfinished business between fathers who die young – Taxi Alex was only 61 and Flying Boat Alex only 67 – their sons unprepared for mourning. Using an automatic timer and positioning the camera on a nearby post, I took a picture of myself by the grave.

Later, with the chill southerly beginning to sweep up the coast, I headed down towards the harbour. Past 37 Wharfe Street, where old roses hanging from the fence seemed to be the only remnant of the house. Did an 11-year-old boy shoot out of the gate in 1927, around the corner into Arun Street, and down the steps and pathways to the bay and wharf in the lee of Cape Wanbrow, marvelling at the news of the American aviator Charles Lindbergh's flight across the Atlantic in his silver monoplane and his hero's welcome in Gay Paree? The harbour and the open Pacific Ocean stretching eastwards towards the Panama Canal and Europe, the strange excitement of big ships and their crews from across the world – this was Lex's playground as a boy. By 1932 'home boats', the Shaw Savill and Union Steam Ship Company refrigerated-cargo liners of nearly 10,000 tons, were using the port.[19]

My father attended Waitaki Boys' High School between 1929 and 1932. He was a day boy, travelling daily up and down the rails his grandfather had helped lay. Waitaki Boys' was in its heyday, with 'The Man', Rector Frank Milner, at the peak of his charismatic powers. James Bertram describes Milner's Waitaki as 'both nursery and shrine to the imperial idea, a regular port of call for visiting admirals and royal dukes'.[20] In 1927 the Hall of Memories had been opened, and staff and pupils gathered for morning assembly in the glow of the East Window: the rich colours of its stained glass lit up by the morning sun. It showed a New Zealand soldier standing alongside Alfred the Great and Richard Coeur de Lion, the Man's selected symbols of English kingly virtue.[21]

But Milner's sense of imperial unity was coupled with an attractively buoyant vision of the new age. He told Rotarians in Boston in 1933 that 'this age concentrates in itself the cumulative energies of the Renaissance, the Reformation, and the Industrial Revolution'. Milner was also a temperance campaigner, though it was later remarked that the ranks of old Waitakians produced a surprising number of determined drinkers.

When Alec brought my mother and us three children back to the southern hemisphere in 1951, we visited Oamaru and my grandmother Mima, whom Alec had not seen since 1937, at 37 Wharfe Street. The house was demolished in the 1960s.[22] I remember also my father taking me to visit Waitaki Boys'. My memory of the occasion is vague, but it must have been a powerful experience for Alec – 20 years on, with so many friends and teachers from the school lost to war.

Figure 12: The Hall of Memories, Waitaki Boys' High School, June 2004.

Returning to Waitaki Boys' in June 2004, I walked across the back field, where the footballers honed their skills in the 1930s, climbed over the rusting wire fence to the rise above the black sand beach and surveyed the sweep of the coast south to Oamaru and Cape Wanbrow and, out front, the greenstone-glistening Pacific Ocean.

Later, I visited the Hall of Memories. Could the boys of my father's generation have suspected as they sat here at assembly, captives of Milner's rhetorical brilliance, that many of their names would, in little more than a decade, join those on the brass plaques recording service in war – many with the asterisk denoting death in service?

The school journal, *The Waitakian*, allows us glimpses of the teenaged Frame: boxing, shooting, 'section commander' in the cadet corps, and playing for the First XV in 1932. On 5 August 1932, on a snow-covered Lancaster Park, the annual encounter between Waitaki and Christchurch Boys' High School was played in sleet and rain. Christchurch downed Waitaki 12–0, but the Christchurch *Press* reported that 'The defence of McKendry, Frame, Dick and Milner was the principal factor in withstanding a series of fierce onslaughts by the Christchurch side'.[23]

The Rector's tone of faithful imperial optimism was not unchallenged. The Head Boy for 1932, Lex's final year, J.M. Paape, was asked to write an editorial on the subject 'What is Youth

Thinking of Modern Problems?' in *The Waitakian* in December 1932. The result was surprisingly forthright:

> The young men of today look about them on a world crippled on the rack of war and threatened by the menace of yet more war. It sees a world bankrupt, with millions of its peoples destitute and starving; it sees nations snapping at nations, peoples rising against peoples; it sees wanton extravagance, and, above all, it sees its school fellows leaving school each year with no possibility of opportunity of work, roaming the streets unemployed and idle – a potential menace. And then youth begins to wonder and to ask what, after all, it has to be grateful for . . .

This defiant analyst, Jack Paape, went on to join the teaching staff at Waitaki in 1937, and was subsequently killed in flying operations over Germany in 1942. It may be that his *cri de coeur* in 1932 better expressed the foreboding and insecurity of his generation as it prepared to enter the adult world than the lofty imperial confidence of the Man. But Milner's defenders could plausibly retort that Paape was precisely a vindication and exemplar of the Rector's ultimate objective: the inculcation of clear-eyed courage.

Milner had done a world tour in 1929 and watched Flight Lieutenant Waghorn fly his dark blue and silver Supermarine S.6 seaplane low over the water at an average speed of 328 miles per hour to win the Schneider Trophy Race at Calshot, the flying-boat base near Southhampton. The aircraft's designer, R.J. Mitchell, was beginning to see in these sleek metal seaplanes the form of his famous Spitfire fighter. The excitement and colour of the event, with the scarlet livery of the Italian entries contrasting with the blue of the British, is recorded at length in Frank Milner's handwritten diary of his world tour:

> Saturday 7 September 1929. Left Brighton at 8 am en route for view of Schneider Trophy Race on Solent . . . Perfectly beautiful day . . . whole competition was intensely thrilling . . . Crowds were moved to intense enthusiasm by the daredevil audacity of the super-airmen . . . Pilots have to be supermen physically and their faculties must be highly sensitive . . . [24]

The Rector recorded that the pilots lost consciousness momentarily, due to the forces created at such speeds in the tight turns of the course. Here was Milner's vision made real: a fusion of athlete and artist! His young Waitakian charges must have been spellbound as the famously eloquent Rector subsequently related these events at morning assembly in the Memorial Hall. Ten years later, the 13-year-old day boy from Oamaru's South Hill who heard this account of far-away wonders would learn the business of flying-boats at Calshot base, the scene of the Schneider Trophy races.

Another spectator that brilliant autumn day at Calshot was an Australian-born pioneer of seaplane aviation, a former commander of Calshot and future RAF chief in the Middle East in 1940–41, Arthur (later Air Chief Marshal Sir Arthur) Longmore, who recorded:

> To see this race, which was run around a triangular course in the Solent, I hired a small Thorneycroft motor-cruiser. We had a splendid view of the race near the turning-point mark boat in Cowes roads . . . The radio commentator on Ryde Pier was giving us news of the race, and when this wild Italian came along low . . . we heard: 'This chap's coming pretty low – by Jove, he is coming low – Good Lord, he's going to hit us'. After which we heard the loud roar of his engine which must have been very close to the microphone.[25]

For Alec, Jack Paape's apprehensive 1932 outburst of gloom was prognostic. On leaving Waitaki in 1933 with university entrance qualifications and aspirations, he found that his meagre income from a job with the Waitaki Dairy Company in Oamaru – making butter, book-keeping, typing, and general office work – was so necessary to his household in a time of economic depression that he could not be spared for further study. His father, the taxi-driver, was by now unemployed. A difficult and frustrating period followed, made bearable only by continuing his rugby career – he played in the North Otago representative team. He also managed to acquire a motorbike on hire-purchase. I remember his telling me rather sheepishly late in life how he had given his name on the contract as 'Emarf' in the hope of concealing the purchase from his disapproving family, but that, when payments fell behind, the repossessors broke this code without difficulty and arrived quite quickly at the Frame residence in Wharfe Street, to his considerable embarrassment.

In the North Island, John Mulgan, another future New Zealand soldier, felt the chilling effect of the depression and would comment:

... the depression was something very big and overwhelming and intangible. People resented it, not only because it did them harm but because they couldn't understand it. It settled on New Zealand like a new and unwanted stranger, a grey and ghastly visitor to the house.[26]

In 1936, a former Mayor of Oamaru, James McDiarmid, summarised the course and effect of these economic conditions:

A boom followed the conclusion of the war for two or three years, then a slowing down up to 1930, an unprecedented slump setting in during the following year. It is said we are emerging from the slump, but today we still find in every town and city of New Zealand hundreds of men and youths in enforced idleness, whose energies are paralysed by an apparent restricted scope for useful employment.[27]

In 1935, just after his nineteenth birthday, and perhaps as a consequence of his cadet corps experience, Alec joined the New Zealand Army's permanent staff, serving at Trentham, near

Figure 13: The Frame family in Oamaru, about 1937. Alex, the taxi-driver, and son 'Lex' – as my father was known in that family – standing. In the front (from left), Auntie May, Grandma 'Mima' (holding Auntie Jess's daughter, Jenny), and Auntie Jess. When Lex left for England and war later that year, he would not see his father again, and his mother and sisters only fourteen years later.

Wellington. He was promoted to corporal in 1937. He specialised in 'weapons training' and played in an army rugby team in 1936.

Lex's big break came in April 1937, when he applied for selection under the 'Short Service Commission Scheme' of the Royal Air Force (RAF). This was an arrangement between the British and New Zealand authorities under which a set number of candidates, chosen after interview and medical examination in New Zealand, would be accepted by the RAF, which then met the cost of their passages to England for training on a four-year commission.[28] Alec's application listed academic and sporting achievements as required. To the question 'Have you ever flown either as a pilot, passenger, or pupil?' he gave a negative answer. His referees were the Rector at Waitaki Boys' High, Frank Milner, and the just-quoted former Mayor of Oamaru, James McDiarmid, who described the candidate in his report as having 'excellent character and attractive personality'.[29] In June 1937 the Air Department notified the success of his application.

Of the 37 applicants selected for the scheme in Alec's batch, more than half (19) would be killed and two more would become prisoners of war.[30] But this grim statistic would have been far from the minds of the young men as they gathered in Auckland for departure: for them, an exciting new world seemed to be opening up.

At 7.25 on the fine early morning of 1 December 1937, Alec sailed from Auckland for Europe on the New Zealand Shipping Company vessel *Ruahine*. Out into the Rangitoto Channel, past Mechanics Bay, where in three weeks would be moored side by side the new Imperial Airways Empire flying boat *Centaurus*, and the ill-fated Pan American Sikorsky S42B *Samoa Clipper* on a route-survey flight. The *Ruahine* was only two days out of Auckland when, on the other side of the world, Captain John W. Burgess, a New Zealander, lifted *Centaurus* off Southampton waters for the first flight to New Zealand. The arrival in Auckland on 27 December was a major national event. Big flying boats were the new thing: their pilots were given civic receptions and treated as film stars.[31]

The passenger list for the *Ruahine* sailing included a group of twelve short-service commission trainees: by 1943 nine of these would be killed in training or in action.[32] Among them, three were destined for flying boats: the other two were C.E.W. Evison, whose career would have similarities to Alec's own,[33] and G.W. Sutton. The journey via the Panama Canal took some five weeks, the party arriving in Britain on 7 January 1938.

Figure 14: Pan American Airways' ill-fated Sikorsky S42B *Samoan Clipper* (Captain Ed Musick) from San Francisco in the foreground, and Imperial Airways' Gouge-designed Short S.23 *Centaurus* (Captain Burgess of New Zealand) from Southampton, moored together off Mechanics Bay, Auckland, having converged in the Waitemata Harbour in December 1937. A new era of international air travel and of flying-boat dominance was beginning. In the background, the double-ended steam ferry *Toroa*, or perhaps its sister-ship *Kestrel*, crosses from Devonport to the city. *Alexander Turnbull Library, Wellington, N.Z., G- 48844-1/4.*

The twelve trainees aboard *Ruahine* were A.S. Dini (killed in a Hurricane after engine failure and a crash near Folkestone on 21 May 1940), F.E. Eustace (killed in a night-fighter attack on his Manchester bomber on 27 June 1941), C.E.W. Evison, A. Frame, C.R. Frankish (killed in his Blenheim bomber when shot down by flak over Belgium on 12 May 1940), B.W. Grieves (killed when his Tiger Moth trainer collided with a fighter plane on 21 January 1938), B.L.G. Harker (killed while training in an Anson on 4 October 1939), G.L.R. Heywood (whose commission ended on 14 July 1938, and who later served with the RNZAF), R.H. Laud (killed when his Stirling bomber was shot down by a night-fighter over Belgium on 12 June 1943), A.S. Luxmoore (killed when his Hampden bomber was brought down by flak over Hanover on 26 June 1940), G.W. Sutton (killed when his Sunderland ran out of fuel and crashed in the sea on 18 September 1939), and K.V. Wendel (died of injuries after his Hurricane was shot down over Kent on 7 September 1940).[34]

Alec's earliest flying training was at the De Havilland Flying

School at Hatfield, near London. The aircraft used was the DH 82A
and the 22-year-old first flew on 17 January 1938. The flying school
had the first batch of ten of these machines, including G-ACDC,
in which Alec flew on 4 February. Remarkably, this aircraft, the
third Tiger Moth produced, is still flying today at the age of 75 with
13,000 hours' flying time to its credit, sporting its maroon and silver
colours in the ownership of the Tiger Club of Great Britain.

Figure 15: De Havilland Flying School, Hatfield, north of London, 1938. Alec is
second from right in front, seated. It is probable that several or all of his *Ruahine*
shipmates from New Zealand are in the picture.

The first reminder to the class that flying was a dangerous
business came four days after Alec's first flight, when shipmate and
fellow trainee B.W. Grieves was killed with his instructor when
Tiger Moth G-ADHW collided with a Gloster Gauntlet fighter near
the aerodrome.

Alec did his first solo flight on 4 February, and completed
the required cross-country return flights to Desford, Ansty, and
Mildenhall in March. I remember his telling me that on those cross-
country flights wide-eyed trainees would desperately look for railway
lines to guide them to their destinations, and sometimes got the
wrong ones, with awkward consequences. Alec was passed out at
the end of March with his 'Proficiency as Pilot' marked 'average'.

The RAF took over the next phase of training at the No 3 Flying
Training School at South Cerney. Now the trainees experienced
service discipline and more powerful aircraft. The machines used
were the single-engined Avro Hart and Audax aircraft, with their

elegantly pointed noses housing Rolls-Royce's water-cooled Kestrel engine. Dundas Bednall, a pilot who trained on these models in the 1930s, remembers them as 'much-loved aircraft . . . huge and demanding':

> Both were pleasant to fly in most circumstances but when inverted, such as when performing slow rolls, the pilot received a large quantity of sand and gravel in his face as the inverted aircraft rid itself of debris accumulated on the floor beneath the pilot.[35]

By August 1938 the instructors were beginning to mark Alec as 'above average'. Specialist training in navigation followed, on twin-engined Anson aircraft at Thorney Island, until in April 1939 Alec received the prized posting to Calshot for flying-boat instruction. Bednall says that the rumour among trainees was that 'the one or two most outstanding pupils might be posted to flying boats, the next bracket to bombers, and the bottom chaps to fighters'.

Calshot, on the Solent near Southampton, had been commissioned as a flying-boat base before World War I. Winston Churchill was aboard the first seaplane flight from there in January 1913. By the 1930s it was the principal flying-boat training base operated by Coastal Command. The earliest hangar, dating from 1913 and nowadays named the 'Sopwith Hangar', and the vast 'Sunderland Hangar' of later vintage, are still there today, serving yachting and rock-climbing enthusiasts. Calshot Castle, built by Henry VIII in 1540 to command the deep-water channel into Southampton, is the central feature at the end of the spit where the slipway launched the RAF trainees and their machines in 1938.

On an early spring morning in 2005, with the sun beginning to penetrate the haze over the Solent (the waters between the English south coast and the Isle of Wight), I visited Calshot Castle, a tower on a pedestal surrounded by a moat, standing guard at the mouth of Southampton Water. Next to it is the slipway from which were launched and recovered the Scapa and Stranraer aircraft on which Alec and his cohort of budding flying-boat pilots trained in 1938–39. They crunched their way across the sea gravel to the jetties and tenders for their earliest encounters with flying boats.

The present Calshot village, on the edge of the New Forest, was the site of the camp, called Eaglehurst, which by 1940 accommodated over 500 trainee airmen. A special baby steam-train – dubbed 'The Calshot Express' – carried personnel from the camp along the spit

Figure 16: Calshot Castle in 2005.

to the operations area around the castle. Alec's first logbook entry for a flying boat was on 25 April 1939, as second pilot in Scapa K4565, when the object was to practice 'seamanship'. A few days later, on 28 April, his first flying-boat solo was in the all-metal Stranraer K7298, and he flew in the same aircraft on 17 May with Pilot Officer Sutton, his compatriot and shipmate from the *Ruahine*. Both the Scapa and the Stranraer were developed by R.J. Mitchell, the brilliant but terminally ill designer of the famous Spitfire fighter, from his earlier Supermarine Southampton flying boat.[36]

The beautiful wooden hull of a Southampton graces the RAF Museum at Hendon, near London. An experienced flying-boat pilot said of these machines: 'If an aeroplane looks good, it almost invariably flies well also, and these did. Everyone knows about the Spitfire's handling but that of these much larger flying boats was also a delight.'[37]

But these elegant bi-planes were about to be made obsolete by the mighty Sunderlands now rolling out of the construction shops of Short Brothers at Rochester. On 8 June 1939 Alec was posted to 210 Squadron at Pembroke Dock on the coast of Wales, and reported there on 19 June. The squadron was led by Wing Commander Daddo-Langlois, inevitably dubbed 'Daddy Longlegs', and Squadron Leader Pearce oversaw flying operations.

Figure 17: Supermarine Stranraer. Alec made his first flying-boat solo flight in this model at Calshot in May 1939.

On 21 June Alec accompanied Pearce in a Mark I Sunderland for the first time – it was L2165. Three 210 Squadron flying boats, including L2165, were positioned at Mount Batten in Plymouth Sound and the next day provided an escort for King George VI and Queen Elizabeth returning home aboard the *Empress of Britain* from a highly successful visit to Canada and the United States, where the royal couple had stayed with the Roosevelts at the White House, establishing an important early transatlantic link on which Roosevelt and Churchill were soon to build. The aviation correspondent of *The Times* reported that 'Flying in one of the aeroplanes from Thorney Island, one had no difficulty in sighting the majestic white vessel against a background of deep green as she moved up the Solent into Southampton water'.[38] 'The Man' at Waitaki Boys' High would have approved of his protégé's minor role in aid of the monarch: here was the East Window in the Memorial Hall come to life in the age of aviation.

On 27 June Alec flew his first Sunderland solo, in L2168. On 8 August he assisted Flight Lieutenant Craven in the delivery of Sunderland L5807 to Pembroke Dock from the Short Brothers' works at Rochester. The log entry for 9 August records Squadron Leader Pearce's certification that Pilot Officer Frame had qualified as 'first pilot/day' for Sunderland Mark I aircraft. Three weeks later war was declared.

Figure 18: Something of the grace, scale, and venomous tail of the Sunderlands is caught in this picture of two 210 Squadron Mark Is being serviced at Oban in 1940.

In these powerful Sunderlands, my father must first have learned the transaction between machine and pilot described by Saint-Exupéry. The pilot

> . . . feels the flying boat second by second as it gathers speed, growing in power. He senses those fifteen tons of metal ripening for flight. The pilot grips the controls and bit by bit takes the power as a gift into the palms of his hands. As the gift is possessed, the metal controls become messengers of his power. When it is fully ripe, and with a movement as deft as the plucking of a fruit, the pilot separates the aircraft from the water and establishes it in the air.[39]

The remarkable Flight Lieutenant Baveystock, who sank two U-boats in 1944, has left us a more prosaic and practical description of wartime Sunderland operations and the teamwork required to prepare the aircraft for take-off. 'Bav' describes the procedure after taxiing to the take-off position in Plymouth Sound off Mount Batten station:

The skipper opened up the outer engines first, at the same time hauling the control column back into his stomach. This allowed the nose of the aircraft to rise as high as possible before opening the throttles of the inner engines. The purpose of this was to cut down the amount of spray from the bow wave that would strike the propellers when the inner engines were opened up. In heavy seas especially, spray would cause 'pitting' of the propeller tips. With the nose at its maximum height, the inner engines were gradually opened up until the props were finally clear of the spray. Full throttle was then given to all four engines. With the aircraft now coming 'onto the step' (in other words, 'planing'), the control column was centralised with the speed reaching about 50 knots. At about 85 to 90 knots the skipper eased back on the stick and the aircraft rose gracefully into the air . . . [40]

4. Flying Boats into War

The development of long-range multi-engined flying boats in the 1930s was connected with the rivalries among three major industrial powers in the provision of airmail services. Governments paid subsidies to their airlines to develop and operate the necessary air routes. A British report gave these figures in pounds sterling for subsidies paid:

	1934–35	1935–36
UK (Imperial Airways)	568,000	430,000
France (Air France)	1,248,000	1,089,000
America (Pan American)	1,215,000	1,644,000

British planners pointed to the deficit, but they had an eye on the strategic and military dimensions also. In April 1935 an internal memorandum at the Air Ministry identified the political implication for the far-flung British Empire: 'The sight of airmail straight from England, arriving two or three times weekly, as regularly as clockwork, must tend to afford a comforting sense of security that England and her squadrons are not so distant after all.'[41] The memorandum assessed the military aspect as well:

> The policy of military air power is virtually that of Napoleon and Clausewitz – rapid concentration of overwhelming strength where needed. In the air that is impracticable, bearing in mind the time factor, without adequate ground facilities and ground organization. The Empire mail routes supply these essentials: in time of peace they are economically employed, and under war conditions are available to promote the smooth and rapid despatch of squadrons from home to the threatened areas.

The document noted that landplane routes across Europe could be disrupted by war, while long-range flying boats promised an 'all-sea route to Gibraltar and the Mediterranean comparatively free from interruption in war'.

In 1933 the Chairman of Imperial Airways, Sir Eric Campbell Geddes, had suggested to the British Cabinet, apparently at the instigation of the company secretary, S.A. Dismore, that the British Government and Imperial Airways investigate the development of airmail on the London–Capetown and London–Australia routes.[42] By December 1936 the British Government was ready to announce in the House of Commons its 'Empire Air Mail Scheme', under which 'all first-class mail matter passing between countries embraced within the British Commonwealth of Nations and served by the Empire air routes shall be sent by air'. The plan contemplated that the British Government would develop the required aircraft for operation by Imperial Airways, and that the governments whose countries were to be served would provide and maintain the necessary ground support. As an example of the time saved by the proposed scheme, the London-Sydney route would be cut from fourteen to seven days. Some countries, New Zealand among them, would not be directly connected and would require separate extensions or surface connections.

But why were flying boats the chosen tool? The British Government set out its reasons in a printed document:

> The flying boat gives greater security over long stretches of water whilst facilitating the comfort of passengers and promoting economy of fuel costs through operating along the sea coast whenever practicable. In particular, it would enable Empire Governments, wherever suitable stretches of water were available for flying boats, to avoid heavy costs of maintaining the surfaces of their land aerodromes at the very high standard required for machines of the weight proposed . . . the scheme visualises such a concentration of the overhaul and repair organization as should preclude the necessity for elaborate ground facilities at intermediate points of call along the flying boat routes.[43]

Flying-boat advocates did not have it all their own way, however. There were doubters in the Air Ministry in London, as this letter in 1937 from the head of Coastal Command, Air Marshal Philip Joubert, reveals:

> I must confess that I am not satisfied by the way in which the Air Staff arguments against flying boats are put forward. They seem to me to be in essence political and technical rather

than a broad appreciation of where the flying boat fits into a well-balanced Air Force . . . My first premise, then, is that, to enable us to operate aircraft everywhere, and on account of our liabilities for reinforcing our air forces overseas at short notice, we must have flying boats.[44]

Pre-war RAF thinking as to the military use of flying boats is explained in an internal paper which, although undated, must have been composed in 1937 or 1938:

Flying Boat Requirements for Metropolitan Air Force

1. The war role assigned to flying boats operating in Home waters is, in co-operation with the Royal Navy, reconnaissance, anti-submarine, and convoy duties. . . .

3. To fulfil this commitment a minimum of 36 flying boats is necessary, on the assumption that each aircraft will fly an average of 60 hours per month . . . .

6. Flying boat squadrons, on account of their mobility, are liable to be the first available to reinforce an overseas garrison on the outbreak of war . . . Hence, at the outbreak of war, it is reasonable to suppose that flying boats will be invaluable as (i) overseas reinforcement (ii) air striking force . . .

9. Of the four new types of flying boat being constructed for the Royal Air Force, only the Sunderland (R.2/33) and the Lerwick (R.1/36) are sufficiently far advanced to merit consideration. Neither of these are yet in service . . . The Sunderland, however, closely resembles the Empire Flying Boat used by Imperial Airways, and consequently it is reasonable to assume that its 'teething' troubles have been overcome.[45]

The outcome of all this interest in flying boats was such that by 1943 the Chief Engineer of Short Brothers at Rochester, C.P.T. Lipscomb, commissioned to advise the New Zealand authorities charged with planning the future air transport needs of the city of Auckland, could conclude that 'At the outbreak of the present war the flying boat had established a position of more or less complete ascendancy over the landplane in British air transport, particularly for the major services linking the Dominions with Great Britain . . . '[46]

The brief but glorious reign of the four-engined flying boat had begun. Although Lipscomb, not perhaps an unbiased observer, conceded that the wartime construction of aerodromes had improved the post-war prospects for landplanes, he urged the Auckland planners that the suitability of flying boats for development in very large sizes would ensure them 'a permanent place in long range air transport'.

The Empire Air Mail Scheme demanded a new long-range flying boat, and tenders were called. Short Brothers of Rochester were likely to be strong candidates, with their extensive experience of flying-boat design and construction dating from 1908. Although some of its medical and ethnological suggestions may be questioned, the following passage from a useful history of the firm sketches the background of the elder of the two brothers:

> Horace (b.1872) had an accident as a child which resulted in meningitis. This led to abnormal brain development, and Horace having an enormous head. It also turned him into something of a genius with a remarkable ability to learn. On leaving school in 1885 he worked with his father in the ironworks. In 1890 he set off on an adventure, sailing for Australia, being shipwrecked in Samoa, captured by cannibals, and worshipped as a King God.[47]

Horace and Oswald Short set up as aircraft manufacturers as early as 1908 and, attracted by the suitability of the river above Rochester bridge for flying-boat operations, began the move to Rochester in 1913. After the initial impetus of World War I, demand for aircraft slackened and the firm had to diversify to keep going. The manufacture of light-weight bus bodies, and even prams, kept the team together. Three metal sailing barges also emerged from the Rochester works.

Arthur Gouge,[48] the son of a Methodist preacher and educated at Gravesend Technical school and Woolwich Polytechnic, joined Short Brothers in 1915 as a mechanic, and worked his way from the shop bench into design leadership, and later directorship, of the company. In 1925 he pioneered a development which gave the firm a decisive edge in flying-boat design: the 'test tank' in which scale models of hulls and floats could be observed under different conditions and improved. Gouge's tank was 300 feet long and featured electrical towing apparatus.

As early as March 1935, Gouge read a paper before the North

East Coast Institution of Engineers and Shipbuilders at Newcastle-on-Tyne. The designer explained the difference between a 'flying-boat' properly so-called, and a mere 'sea-plane': the first had a fuselage or hull designed especially for travel through water; the second was an aeroplane attached to floats. Gouge continued:

> From the earliest days of flying, designers have been interested in the problem of building aircraft which would alight on or take-off from the water and although the development of the marine aircraft may not have been quite so spectacular as has been the case in the land type, yet steady progress has been maintained for many years past. In fact, it is more than probable that the future of large aeroplanes will be largely bound up with the development of the flying-boat.[49]

Figure 19: This portrait of the 48-year-old Arthur Gouge at the peak of his career, taken in 1938 by Bassano, is in the National Portrait Gallery in London. *The Times* obituary on 16 October 1962 stated that 'Both the Sunderland for the RAF and the Empire flying-boat for Imperial Airways evolved under his guidance . . . He was a stocky, solid man, blessed with a steady common sense and the ability to push an undertaking through with vigour and a sure touch . . . '

Gouge's paper went on to consider several design problems for flying-boat construction. One of these was the need to keep the aircraft upright and stable in the water. It is clear from the paper that Gouge was already thinking not only of four-engined aircraft of about 50,000 pounds with wing-spans of about 100 feet, such as the forthcoming Empire and Sunderland boats, but of much larger flying boats powered by as many as ten engines, weighing in excess of 300,000 pounds, and with wing-spans of over 200 feet, such as the giant Gouge-designed Saunders-Roe Princess which would first fly in 1952. Three basic configurations for achieving the necessary lateral stabilisation were considered. They were:

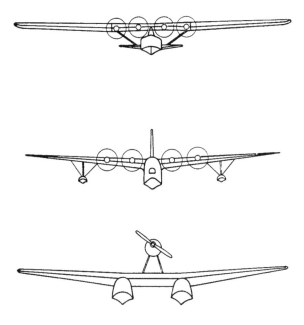

Figure 20: Diagram from Arthur Gouge's 1935 paper. The middle configuration is already recognisably that of the Empire and Sunderland flying boats.

The first model, with 'sponsons' projecting laterally from the hull, was favoured by the German designer Claude Dornier, and was later used also by the American Boeing 314 Clippers. The third, the twin-hulled model, was chosen by Italian flying-boat makers such as Savoia-Marchetti, whose squadron of SM 55 aircraft had flown the South Atlantic under the dashing Italo Balbo's command in 1930. The second model, using wing-mounted floats, is recognisably that of Gouge's Empire boats and the Sunderland. Gouge himself pronounced in his 1935 Newcastle lecture: 'In our opinion . . . the wing-tip float is the best all-round compromise as it is lighter, causes less interference with the hull during take-off, and its parasitic drag is less than the alternative methods.'[50]

This verdict rested on Gouge's experience with his trump card as a designer, the test-tank:

> It is impossible, at the moment, to predict the stability characteristics of any flying-boat hull from theoretical considerations only . . . From my own experience, after many years of intensive tank work, it has become clear that when a model of a flying-boat hull has been completely tested and cured of any instability troubles, then it can reasonably be expected that no trouble will occur in full size.[51]

By March 1936 tank tests were being carried out by the Royal Aircraft Establishment at Farnborough on a 1:15 scale model to explore the planing stability and take-off time and distance of the Sunderland hull. The conclusions were that stability would be satisfactory, and that the windless take-off time would be 19.7 seconds and the length of the run 435 yards. The only recommendation was that 'a small movement of the main step aft would be an improvement'.[52]

Kenneth Poolman's pioneering study *Flying Boat*[53] suggests that Gouge's design was a response both to the Air Ministry's requirements for a new four-engined military flying boat, and to the Imperial Airways specification for the mail-carrying civil flying boat. Phillip Sims's recent and equally valuable work also notes the convergence on Gouge's drawing-board of the civil specification for Imperial Airways needs and the RAF's specification issued in 1933.

> Gouge noted similarities in the two specifications and produced a common design. At the close of 1934, to meet the [civil] specification, Short Bros tendered to Imperial the Short S.23. They received an 'instruction to proceed' in late January 1935. First delivery was to be April 1936. A large design staff was employed and the first metal must have been cut by early summer 1935.[54]

Poolman adds that Gouge's preference for all-metal construction was reinforced by a visit in October 1934 to the gathering at Mildenhall, in Suffolk, of aircraft entered in the Empire Air Race to Australia: the DC2 – precursor of the famed DC3 workhorse – impressed Gouge with its uncompromising metal construction.[55] His subsequent design work was so good that Shorts obtained an order for 27 machines straight off the drawings. One innovation in Gouge's design was his invention of a fully retractable trailing-edge flap which allowed more lift as well as a slower landing speed.

In his 1935 Newcastle paper, Arthur Gouge had discussed the choice of engines for flying boats:

> 'The two types, namely water-cooled and air-cooled, have progressed almost side-by-side, but of late years there appears to a definite leaning towards the air-cooled type largely on account of its simplicity and ease of maintenance.'[56]

The power plant selected by Short Brothers for their new flying boats was the Bristol Aeroplane Company's Pegasus – a nine-cylinder, radial, air-cooled engine, developed from the company's Jupiter and Mercury engines of the 1920s. The 1010 horsepower Pegasus XXII was the model installed in the Mark I Sunderland. The Pegasus engine was persisted with for Sunderlands until its replacement, pioneered by the Australian 10 Squadron, by the more powerful and reliable American Pratt and Whitney engines in the Mark V Sunderland in 1944.

Although generally reliable, the Pegasus was found to be prone to failure of cylinder valves. These were operated by rocker-boxes lubricated by oil pads on top of each cylinder: in hot climates, such as those experienced in the Mediterranean and West Africa, it was found that the lubrication deteriorated, leading to cylinder and engine failure. The problem was compounded by the circumstance that the propellers could not be 'feathered' and would therefore continue to spin in the airflow even on a dead or burning engine, making damage control difficult and endangering the aircraft.

The first S.23 or 'Empire Boat', *Canopus*, bearing the registration G-ADHL, was rolled out on the slipway at Rochester on 1 July 1936 and the engines tested. On the following day the flying boat was launched into the Medway and moored with the intention of attempting a first flight on Saturday 4 July. Sims relates how the day before, Shorts' test pilot, John Lankester Parker, initially intending only 'fast taxiing', allowed the aircraft to become airborne for fourteen minutes. The projected 'first flight' duly took place the next day:

Lankester Parker returned over Rochester Castle and the works, put *Canopus* into a steep climbing starboard turn, and sped down the Medway valley. Moments later he swept down before the assembled work force. This was the pre-arranged signal to Oswald Short and Gouge, who thankfully lit a cigarette, that all was well.[57]

That test pilot, John Lankester Parker, must have been the 'J.L.P.' who wrote to *The Times* following Gouge's death in 1962, to add his tribute to his old designer's memory. He said of 'A.G', as his colleagues knew him, that he had a

> special quality ... which endeared him to the test pilots privileged to work with him ... It was the absolute faith and trust he placed in them without any regard for the tone of their criticism, either pleasing or unexpected. Such faith was naturally reciprocated in full measure and may well have played an important part in his success.[58]

The Sunderland was in effect an Empire Boat with gun turrets at each end. The prototype, K4774, flew for the first time on 16 October 1937. By April 1938, Lankester Parker was flight-testing the first of the original seven production machines.

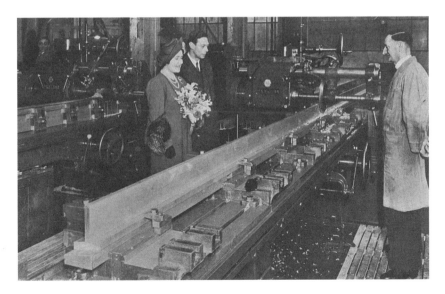

Figure 21: King George VI and Queen Elizabeth at Shorts in Rochester on 14 March 1939, watching a Sunderland main spar emerge from a giant lathe.

On 14 March 1939, as Hitler swallowed up Czechoslovakia, revealing even to British Prime Minister Neville Chamberlain that the Munich agreement had been a futile sop to the dictator, the King and Queen visited the Short Brothers works in Rochester and were shown all phases of design and construction. *The Times* reported:

> They watched blue-prints being made. They saw aircraft parts being beaten into shape with a mallet or machined to precise limits or being fitted together in jigs ... In the course of their walk they talked to many of the men and girls in their overalls ... Their Majesties passed through the little workshop where aircraft models have been made for years, and next stopped to ask questions about the long tank in which model hulls are tested. Then, almost without warning, they found themselves in the big assembly shops where flying-boat hulls, rising almost to the high roof, and tall scaffoldings gave the impression of a set of stocks at an indoor shipyard.[59]

Figure 22: The shop floor at Shorts in Rochester, on the occasion of the royal visit in March 1939. A Sunderland is under construction in the centre. The company maintained progressive industrial policies.

The King and Queen, the latter dressed in a violet costume and hat trimmed with fur, were shown the three Golden Hind flying boats under construction, and then the smaller C Class Empire boats, *Awarua* and *Australia*, intended for the trans-Tasman run.

Finally, the royal pair bent low to enter the hatch of a Sunderland nearing completion and walked the length of the hull, noting the armaments and internal layout. Arthur Gouge then escorted the royal couple out to the apron fronting the River Medway, where an umbrella was produced to protect the Queen from the drizzling rain. On cue, Lankester Parker started up a new Mark I Sunderland: 'the four engines began to roar and the flying-boat moved steadily away and, lifting off the water, climbed over Rochester Bridge'.

Figure 23: The senior staff at Short Brothers, Rochester. In the front row, third from left, is Arthur Gouge. The tall figure holding a hat in the centre is H.O. Short. The chief test-pilot, J. Lankester Parker, is holding a pipe on the far right, front row.

Meanwhile, political events of great significance were unfolding in Europe. On the evening of the royal visit to Rochester, Winston Churchill, MP, whose campaign to resist Nazi expansion was gathering momentum, spoke at Waltham Abbey in Essex, telling his audience that 'The great and growing German Army is now free to turn in any direction: we do not know in what direction it will turn.' *The Times* editorial on the same day reviewed the events in Czechoslovakia and opined: 'more and more the Nazi Reich appears to be determined not only to expand to its full stature, but also to extend its domination wherever the weakness of other nations may seem to make the extension possible'.

Understandably, attention now turned from the glamorous

Empire Boats of Imperial Airways and their exotic routes and celebrity-filled salons, to the more prosaic military Sunderland, which could offer protection against submarines, conduct armed reconnaissance, maintain links with the Empire, and carry political and military leaders to Cairo without overflying foreign territory. Poolman records that each Sunderland cost the Treasury £80,000 – very roughly £2.2 million sterling or $NZ6.8 million in 2004 equivalents.[60] When war broke out in September 1939, RAF Coastal Command had 27 Mark I Sunderlands in service. Over the period of the war, more than 800 Sunderlands in Marks I to V would be built.

Figure 24: The prototype Mark I Sunderland.

The best record of a Mark I Sunderland moored, taxiing, at take-off, and in flight is perhaps found in the 1942 film *Coastal Command*.[61] I did not know this on May Day 2003 as I walked out of Lambeth North tube station in South London, past the great palace of Henry VIII's time, now housing the Imperial War Museum fronted by its massive grey twin naval gun barrels, to the red brick annexe which serves as the museum's photograph and film archive. By appointment, I had come to view the 70-minute wartime film. As usual, my interest had been sparked by an entry in Alec's logbook, this one made at Oban on the west coast of Scotland: '12 July 1942

. . . self and P/O Rees . . . Sunderland L2160 . . . Local film work . . . 3.40 hours'. Surely, this must refer to the Crown Film Unit's 1942 production?

The film was soon set up by helpful curators, and good-quality black-and-white images were moving to the sound of Ralph Vaughan-Williams's specially written score, gifted to the production by the composer. The story-line and its telling are a little simple – borderline propaganda in fact. Flying boats on patrol attack an enemy submarine with depth-charges and later search for a German raider in the North Atlantic. The raider is found and, by splendid co-ordination between the RAF and the Royal Navy – and plucky flying – tracked, bombed, and sunk. *Coastal Command* focuses on one Sunderland crew and its amiably cool, moustachioed, pipe-smoking skipper. Some of its dialogue will seem to a modern audience a little stilted and almost a caricature of the World War II RAF type. However, real pilots and crews play the parts, and senior Coastal Command officers of the time also appear in control-room scenes.[62]

The film has two endearing features: one is Vaughan-Williams's powerful score, accompanying the action with ethereal, lugubrious passages, and building some powerful and appropriate climaxes. The other is the superb aerial photography, including extended sequences of Mark I Sunderlands variously at mooring, being loaded, taxiing, and then opening the Pegasus engines up to full power to bring the boat on to the step and up into the dawn sky. One spectacular sequence shows a Sunderland low over the town of Bowmore on the island of Islay, almost among the low roofs and narrow streets, and over the Round Church. There are shots of a Sunderland in flight in which the registration number can be clearly seen: L2160, the early production Mark I Sunderland noted in Alec's logbook entry for 12 July. Although Alec does not appear in the film, it is clear that he was one of the several pilots to have flown Sunderlands for these demanding film-makers.

Neil Owen is today both a police inspector at Oban and the leading authority on the Sunderland squadrons at Oban during the war. He can identify many of the airmen and officers appearing in *Coastal Command*, recounting that during the making of the film the 228 Squadron officers, almost certainly including Alec, formed a guard of honour at the Round Church in Bowmore for the wedding of their comrade, Joe Grunert. He wrote to me in 2006 that 'the film is regularly shown on Islay – it is seen as part of the island's heritage now'.

Pembroke Dock is the end of the line, the westernmost railhead in Pembrokeshire in Wales. During the war years it hosted the largest operational flying-boat station in the world, sheltering dozens of Sunderlands and other flying boats at a time. My train from Salisbury slowed to a stop there on 8 May 2003, and soon I was installed in the excellent 'Bed and Breakfast' of Anne and Bill Robinson.

Figure 25: Pembroke Dock, taken from the post-war Cleddau bridge, May 2003. The two big Sunderland hangars are the most visible reminders of wartime flying-boat days.

Pembroke Dock was the creation of the Royal Dockyards, established there in 1814, and the construction site of more than 250 ships, including the largest ever three-deck man-o'-war, the *Duke of Wellington*, in 1852. The yard closed in 1926, but its slipways were inherited by the flying-boat squadrons in 1930. The asset which made 'PD' – as the flying boat men came affectionately to call it – attractive for large boat-building and flying-boat operations alike was the adjoining Milford Haven. This submerged river valley, formed at the end of the last ice age when the sea level rose, offered a deep, protected, inland harbour – ideal for both activities.

I had arranged to meet at Pembroke Dock the air historian and chronicler of flying-boat squadrons, John Evans. This amiable and scholarly Welshman generously agreed to give me a conducted tour of the former flying-boat base and its surrounds. The solid grey stone construction of the entrance gates – guarded no doubt in wartime – and mess and office buildings were a legacy from the Royal Dockyards and gave a feeling of permanence and solidity. Two massive hangars with giant rolling doors, each capable of housing three Sunderlands, provide the most vivid remaining trace of the Sunderlands at Pembroke Dock.

Figure 26: 'Three Colonial Airmen' was the caption on this photograph taken by the official RAF photographer, Stanley Devon, at Oban in early August 1940. Flight Lieutenant Frame is in the middle. On the right, in forage cap, is fellow New Zealander, Pilot Officer (later Wing Commander and DFC) T.P. Gibson. The airman on the left appears to be the Australian, Ivor Meggitt.

On 19 June 1939, Pilot Officers Evison, Frame, and Sutton – all New Zealanders[63] – reported to 210 Squadron from the Flying Boat Training School at Calshot. Within days they were introduced to the new Sunderlands. A week after the declaration of war, on 11 September, came the first taste of one of the Sunderland's most typical roles, when Alec, in L2165, was sent to assist the vessel *Blairlogie* under U-boat attack. Four and a half hours out from PD, the Sunderland found the crew in life boats, guided an American vessel to the scene, and stood by until the rescue was made. They returned to base late in the evening after a ten-hour flight over 1300 miles. The satisfaction of a successful rescue, of survivors plucked from the unforgiving sea, must have been real.[64]

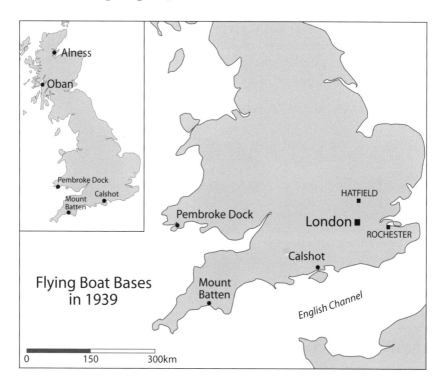

Flying Boat Bases in 1939

However, a week later another aspect of the new war presented itself. On 17 September, the same L2165, under Flight Lieutenant Davies and with Pilot Officers Sutton and Brant, took off from PD on anti-submarine patrol. The squadron's Operations Record Book (ORB) takes up the story:

> Returning at night, the aircraft failed to find Pembroke Dock, & D/F [direction finding] bearings were requested and obtained. The bearings given indicated that the aircraft was over the Irish Sea and when St. Ann's lighthouse was found the petrol supply must have been exhausted, & the aircraft crashed in the sea at the entrance of Milford Haven 0030. All lives lost.[65]

The precariousness of life in war, the vital importance of navigation, and the fragility of the aircraft's hull as a cocoon of warmth and safety, needing only one error, or stroke of ill luck, to be torn open in a second, must have been brought home painfully to the 'new boys' of 210 Squadron as they coped with the deaths of their comrades, including Sutton of their intake, with whom Alec had flown in Stranraers at Calshot.

A favourite song of my father's was the 'Ten Green Bottles' song. He taught my sisters and me to sing it when we were little in Tahiti days and used to gather in our parents' bed when we awoke in the morning:

Ten green bottles, a' hanging on the wall (repeat)
And if one green bottle, should accidentally fall
They'll be nine green bottles, a' hanging on the wall

Figure 27: Captain Maurice (Mauri) McGreal, Auckland, April 2004.

And so on, with numbers getting lower. Mauri McGreal confirms my impression that this and similar songs had a wartime mess background. He reminded me in a conversation in Auckland in April 2004 of another taught to us by Alec in those tropical morning sessions – 'Green grow the rushes oh, who'll give me a three oh' – and comments that these were among the old English pub songs which 'were part of the boozy sing-songs in many messes from the Airmen's up to the Officers. They grew out of the interwar years 1919–1939 on RAF stations in the lonely desert stations of Mesopotamia.'

The expression 'to go for a Burton', signifying death by misadventure, was one that I picked up from my father, and used without consciousness of its origin as explained by Captain McGreal in his account of wartime flying: Burtons was a well-known ale and 'a few pints downed by the lads who were left and a jolly ribald song that told of the joy of living and of the pleasure of pretty girls, was often the only obituary most airmen had'.[66] This transformation of grief and mourning into a kind of collective play – in song and slang – seems to have been how these young men, little more than teenagers, coped with the fact of death in their midst.

Figure 28: 210 Squadron mascot, 'Susie', poses with pilots for Stanley Devon at Oban, 31 July 1940. On the left is Stan Baggott, then Alec, T.P. Gibson, and on the right Ivor Meggitt.

One of the most attractive capacities of the Sunderland was its endurance in flight. The operational characteristics of prototype K4774 were extensively studied by the Marine Aircraft Experimental Establishment at Felixstowe in 1938, and the testers reported in January 1939.[67] The main fault found was that the pilot's canopy leaked badly in even moderate rain. Other conclusions were that the aircraft could be refuelled to its maximum of 2000 gallons in 20 minutes, take-off distance was 680 yards, fuel consumption was 285 gallons per hour, and maximum speeds of 165 knots at 500 feet and 182 knots at 6000 feet could be attained. The most economical speed was about 130 knots at 2000 feet, which produced a fuel consumption of 110 gallons per hour, an endurance of 18 hours, and a coverage of 2750 air miles.

Figure 29: 210 Squadron's Mark I Sunderland L2163 frozen in flight by Stanley Devon's camera, July 1940.

Endurance and range were thus significant features of the new machines. One of the most important limitations was the ability of the crew, and particularly the aircraft commander, to remain alert for long periods of flight. In 1941 the RAF asked its medical experts to investigate the possible use of the stimulant Benzedrine to enhance the wakefulness of its flight crews. This was the task of the Flying Personnel Research Committee, whose reports on the matter may be found in the British National Archives. The committee tested Benzedrine on flight crews, stipulating that subjects should be told merely that the tablets were 'to help them in their flying' and that further questions should be dealt with by 'cheerful evasion'. Among the results recorded was 'Interference with the time sense . . . time seeming to pass much more quickly for a subject under Benzedrine, and one man complained that the drug made him feel "lustful".' Crews reported difficulty in sleeping after Benzedrine-assisted missions, but the committee offered a solution: 'There should be no hesitation in combating it with a quick-acting drug such as Hexobarbitone.'[68]

The committee reported in May 1941 that

> Benzedrine sulphate tablets produce a general feeling of well-being and of increased confidence, and they lessen normal feelings of weariness in the majority of adults . . . There is no evidence that Benzedrine in 5–10 mg doses impairs judgment, skill, either mental or physiological, or adversely affects co-ordinated muscular effort . . . If tablets are taken the effects come on in about one hour and persist for a marked degree for about 8 hours . . . [69]

A further study was undertaken, leading to a report in August 1941 noting that Benzedrine was in any case beginning to be obtained and 'surreptitiously' used by aircrew, and commenting that 'its official sanction under medical supervision would clear up a situation which at present is unsatisfactory':

> The intelligent use of this drug in selected cases to keep pilots alert and awake is justified. With the exception of the captain of the aircraft . . . all other members of the crew are able to take adequate periods of rest and can sleep on the bunks provided for this purpose. In practice a keen captain rarely, if ever, takes a rest, for when he is not actively flying the aircraft, he is checking the navigation. Since he is finally responsible for all that happens he never reaches a state of mind conducive to rest . . . It is therefore the captain of the aircraft who would benefit the most by the judicious use of Benzedrine . . . Two tablets of 5 mg each were given during flight with beneficial results to selected pilots.[70]

These records suggest that Benzedrine was probably in use, whether officially or 'surreptitiously', by at least some Sunderland captains and crew on long patrols and missions. The effect on pilots of the drugs recommended by RAF medical advisers is another factor to be reckoned with in any attempt to understand the conditions experienced by pilots.

The 210 Squadron ORB[71] shows that many long endurance sorties were carried out by its Sunderlands and their crews in late 1939 and 1940. Three under Alec's command may be mentioned as showing Sunderlands performing the sort of work for which they had been intended.

The first, early in the war: '10 October 1939: Sunderland L2163 (Frame, Meggitt, Lamond) carried out a search north of the Faroe Islands for units of the enemy navy . . . 0655-1615'. L2163 was one of the earliest production Sunderlands. This is the first appearance in the logbook of the New Zealand team of Frame and Henry Lamond, the latter of whom is the subject of interview in Chapter 8.

Another, in May 1940:

> 12 May 1940: L2163 (Frame, Meggitt, Phillips) carried out an anti-submarine escort, with a damaged destroyer, HMS Kelly, under tow. Convoy was approx. 100 miles E. of Firth of Forth and when sighted it had just been attacked by 6 Heinkels and 1 Junkers 88. Enemy a/c disappeared and were not seen again. Weather good. Left convoy 2035 and moored up at Invergordon 2330.

The *Kelly* was Lord Louis Mountbatten's destroyer: it had been torpedoed by a German E-boat in the North Sea on 9 May, leaving many casualties and a 40-foot hole in its side from the waterline to the keel. Under desperate tow, the *Kelly* was again attacked from the air over the next three days, but finally made it to the Tyne shipyards for repair. The refitted *Kelly* would finally be sunk by German dive-bombers off the south coast of Crete a year later. Alec's logbook recording one of the protective missions in aid of the *Kelly* shows the Sunderland as having been in the air for 11 hours and 20 minutes.

Their comrade on the flight deck, Flight Lieutenant I. H. Meggitt, was killed on 27 December 1940 when, returning in the dark from convoy escort, Sunderland N9022 hit debris (bizarrely, a partly submerged horse-float from a bombed cargo ship) while attempting to alight at Oban. The aircraft broke up and ten of the eleven crew members, including Ivor Meggitt, died in the freezing water.

A third entry from Alec's logbook relates to assistance given to the torpedoed ship *Empire Merchant*:

> 16 August 1940: L2163: at 14.08 sighted 3 lifeboats, estimated 30-40 survivors [of the *Empire Merchant*]. Photos taken. At 15.40 hrs a/c attempted to alight, but damaged starboard float and took off again. Gave position of lifeboats and alighted Oban 17.45.

Although flying-boat pilots are generally tolerant of popular misconceptions about the capacities of their aircraft, they can be impatient with the belief that flying boats are capable of alighting on the open sea in practically all conditions. In fact, open-sea landings are problematic in even moderate swells. Apart from the dangers of wave impact to the hull, even damage to floats can mean that the aircraft loses stability as it slows on the water and may sink. In this case, L2163 took off again before losing speed and stability on the water. Techniques are available in sheltered alighting areas to shift weight to protect a damaged float, sometimes by placing crew members on the opposite wing once the aircraft is taxiing on the water, and it must be surmised that some such procedure was employed on L2163's return to Oban.[72]

As 210 Squadron explored the versatility of its Sunderlands, momentous changes were occurring in the leadership of the war effort. On 10 May 1940, Churchill became Prime Minister and made his 'blood, toil, tears and sweat' speech in House of Commons.[73]

General 'Pug' Ismay, head of the Chiefs of Staff Committee, recalled the emotional, even unstable, aspect of the new PM's temperament:

> Two or three days after he became Prime Minister I walked with him from Downing Street to the Admiralty. A number of people waiting outside the private entrance greeted him with cries of 'Good luck, Winnie, God bless you.' He was visibly moved, and as soon as we were inside the building, he dissolved into tears. 'Poor people,' he said, 'poor people. They trust me, and I can give them nothing but disasters for quite a long time'.[74]

The PM himself recalled of the period that 'There was a white glow, overpowering, sublime, which ran through our island from end to end'.[75]

While the pilots of Fighter Command – Churchill's famous 'few' – battled the Luftwaffe over southern England in the summer of 1940, Coastal Command's Sunderlands continued the less glamorous, but demanding, search and rescue work.

5. T9046 Goes to the Mediterranean

On 22 November 1940 the Frame/Lamond team was given the task of air-testing and delivering to 228 Squadron in Malta a new Mark I Sunderland hot off Arthur Gouge's Rochester production line. It bore the registration T9046, and would become very much Alec's personal aircraft for the next ten months. Henry Lamond told me in 2003 that he and Alec thought they would be returning to Pembroke Dock after delivery of T9046 and that they were rather 'shanghaied' into the 228 Squadron force in Malta. The 228 Squadron ORB on 4 December 1940 recorded:

> A new aircraft – T9046 – allotted to the Squadron from UK proceeded from Mount Batten to Gibraltar. The aircraft was flown by Fl. Lt. Frame and F/O Lamond who have been posted to Squadron from No. 210 Squadron. The crew consisted of personnel who formed part of the detachment who remained in UK since last June. [76]

The final sentence confirms that the crew were part of the Pembroke Dock detachment of 228 Squadron rather than the Malta component. But hard-pressed Malta needed them more than 'home waters', and in the 'Med' they stayed.

Ernle Bradford tells us in his fine history of the Mediterranean that

> The name Malta stems from the Phoenician word *malat*, a harbour, haven, or place of refuge. This it must certainly have seemed to these early navigators, who came across it lonely in the middle of the sea, standing at the cross-roads of the trade routes, on the dividing line between eastern and western basins. [77]

A thousand years before the time of Christ, the Phoenicians had made use of Malta. The disciple Paul was shipwrecked there in 58 AD at the entrance to what is today called Saint Paul's Bay. Charged by the Jewish authorities in Jerusalem with 'many and grievous complaints' and brought before the Roman court in Caesarea, Paul exercised his right to appeal to Caesar Augustus in Rome. On his way there under guard, soon after passing Crete, his ship was caught in a great storm, the effects of which are recorded in the Bible:

> And when neither sun nor stars in many days appeared, and no small tempest lay on us, all hope that we should be saved was then taken away . . .
>
> And falling into a place where two seas met, they ran the ship aground; and the forepart stuck fast, and remained unmoveable, but the hinder part was broken with the violence of the waves.
>
> And the soldiers' counsel was to kill the prisoners, lest any of them should swim out and escape.
>
> But the centurion, willing to save Paul, kept them from their purpose; and commanded that they which could swim should cast themselves first into the sea, and get to land;
>
> And the rest, some on boards, and some on broken pieces of the ship. And so it came to pass, that they escaped all safe to land . . . .
>
> And when they were escaped, then they knew that the island was called Melita.
>
> And the barbarous people shewed us no little kindness: for they kindled a fire, and received us every one, because of the present rain, and because of the cold.[78]

In 'Melita' for three months, Paul repaid the hospitality of his hosts by healing the father of the chief Publius before resuming his journey to Rome.

Bradford speculates that Malta was 'Ogygia', the island home of Homer's amorous nymph-goddess, Calypso, the detainer of Odysseus for seven years. Only the intervention of Hermes at the behest of the great Zeus persuaded Calypso to allow the object of her desires to return to his wife, Penelope, although the long-suffering hero was induced to endure a night of love-making with his captrix to seal his release.

Malta's strategic position commanding the narrow passage beween Sicily and Tunisia in the central Mediterranean ensured it a constant importance throughout the Greek and Roman eras, and in 1523 the island became the home of the ferociously militant Christian Order of Saint John, the last redoubt against the all-conquering Turkish Empire and its Ottoman fleet. On that redoubt the great

Suleiman's wave faltered in 1565, when the knights of Saint John under their Grand Master, La Vallete, withstood for four months the 40,000 men and 200 ships of the Turkish attack, so turning the tide of Ottoman supremacy in the Mediterranean.

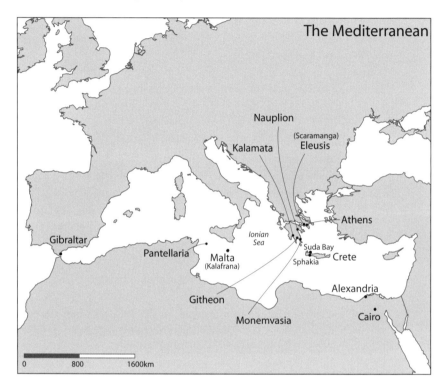

A glance at the map will show how Malta commanded the vital supply lines of both contenders for control of the Mediterranean in 1941. The British artery through the straits of Gibraltar to Wavell's hard-pressed forces in Egypt, and German support from Sicily for what would soon be Rommel's benzene-thirsty Afrika Korps in Libya, were both vulnerable to attack at this point.

Kalafrana Bay, at the south-west end of Malta, was a British flying-boat station of long standing. The station was built in 1916 for World War I purposes, and extensively used in the 1920s and 30s both as a base for RAF squadrons and as a staging point for military and civil long-range flying boats. The principal base was at the mouth of Marsaxlokk (pronounced 'Marsa-shlock') Bay and had a protective camber as shelter against the often violent winds and swells of the *gregale*, the strong cold north-east wind of the central Mediterranean. The flying-boat moorings were placed deeper in the bay, off the fishing village of Marsaxlokk itself. For the same meteorological reason, a secondary and alternative alighting area with some support facilities was established in the sheltered Saint Paul's Bay on the north coast near the eastern end of Malta.

Figure 30: Marsaxlokk Bay in 2005. The tower on the hill, the slipway now crowded with fishing boats, and the Sunderland hangar on the right were all part of the wartime flying-boat station.

The flight of Sunderland T9046 to Malta in 1940 was not without problems, as Henry Lamond told me in the interview recounted later in this book. It took ten hours to fly from Mount Batten base in Plymouth to Gibraltar – partly at night to avoid German fighters in the Bay of Biscay. The final seven-hour leg from Gibraltar to Malta was flown on 6 December 1940, on which date the 228 Squadron ORB recorded that 'T9046 arrives in Malta at 1500 hours. Passengers G. Capt. Pelly, Dr Atkinson, and six Squadron airmen.'[79]

December 1940 was the coldest month recorded in Malta for seventeen years. After three days' rest – and presumably with the news having been broken that they were there to stay – the new boys on the squadron were doing 'local practice' and 'low level bombing practice' under the supervision of a pair of old hands, Flight Lieutenants McKinley and Glover, another Kiwi.[80] Soon, as

1940 came to an end, the Frame/Lamond team were flying ten-hour patrols in T9046 over the Ionian sea.

The new year began badly for T9046 when, on 3 January, a heavy swell and wind in Kalafrana Bay made the aircraft snatch fiercely at its moorings:

> T9046 broke loose first pulling out its pennant eye-piece and then snapping its anchor chain. The boatguard, Sergeant Broomhead, doped up the engines and started two of them and taxied the flying boat, thus preventing its running aground . . . Full crews slept on board and continuous watch was kept throughout the night . . . [81]

The next day, T9046 and other damaged flying boats were debombed and defuelled and brought up the slip at Marsaxlokk, where the ground crews worked around the clock to repair the extensive damage.[82] This was completed by 10 January.

In January 1941, Admiral Andrew Browne Cunningham and his Mediterranean fleet were in a desperate struggle to protect from the attacks of Italian and German naval and air forces the British 'Operation Excess' convoys trying to supply Malta and Egypt. On 11 January, T9046 (Frame, Lamond, Austin) flew a twelve-hour reconnaissance patrol during which sightings were made of a French hospital ship, then of a precious 'Excess' convoy, and finally of Admiral Cunningham's battle fleet itself. The ORB records that the Sunderland received visual signals from the admiral's flagship *Warspite* to patrol a nearby sector 'to limit of endurance'. At 12.33, Cunningham flashed a long visual signal, 'Most Secret Immediate Message for Admiralty', sending the Sunderland back to Malta with it.

This laborious method of communication, no doubt using the Aldis lamp with which messages could be flashed in Morse code, is an interesting comment on the crucial role of communications and security at the time. Clearly, Admiral Cunningham was unwilling to risk breaking radio silence, so revealing his presence and position to the enemy as the cat-and-mouse game unfolded. Alec's report in the ORB noted that 'Time taken to pass, receive, and repeat back message by V.S. [visual signal] 65 minutes (53 groups)'.

Andrew Browne Cunningham – 'ABC' was the inevitable sobriquet – might have been a New Zealander had his father's application for the Chair of Anatomy at the University of Otago in the 1870s been successful. Now, the admiral was engaged in serious

thinking on the bridge of the *Warspite*. A day earlier, the aircraft-
carrier *Illustrious* had encountered the strike power of the newly
arrived Luftwaffe, and had now limped, shattered, back into Malta.
Cunningham had witnessed the devastation at close quarters from
his flagship and seen the capacity of the Stuka dive-bombers to hit
ships from the air.

Figure 31: Reconnaissance photograph taken by Sunderland T9046, 11 January
1941, probably with F24 camera. The border note identifies the subject as a
'French Hospital Ship'.

The admiral was a 'hands on' commander:

> In the *Warspite* I carried out my usual routine. I never took
> my clothes off at sea except for my daily bath, and never
> left the close proximity of the bridge. I had a sea cabin and
> bathroom one ladder down, and here I had my meals unless
> some urgent situation compelled me to have them in the
> Commander-in-Chief's charthouse on the bridge.[83]

Cunningham gives his own account of his position on the night of
10 January:

> During the night we withdrew to the eastward, covering
> the convoy. We had plenty to think about. In a few minutes
> the whole situation had changed. At one blow the fleet had
> been deprived of its fighter aircraft, and the command of
> the Mediterranean was threatened by a weapon far more
> efficient and dangerous than any against which we had
> fought before.[84]

This alarming assessment was no doubt the subject matter of the
message laboriously flashed to the circling Sunderland for the
Admiralty.

On 12 January, T9046 flew from Malta in the night. The logbook
gives the destination as 'special mission – Gulf of Hammamet'.
Unusually, the squadron's commander, Wing Commander
Nicholetts,[85] was aboard, although Alec's log records himself as
'first pilot', indicating that he was at the controls. There were '2
passengers'. A guess must be that the mission was connected with
one of Churchill's favourite projects of the period, 'Operation
Workshop'. Churchill tells us that in September 1940 he conceived
the plan to use a commando attack to seize the Italian island of
Pantelleria, lying in the Gulf of Hammamet off the Tunisian coast.
By December the Prime Minister was pressing his staff, as in this
minute exemplifying the extraordinary verbal style with which
Churchill ran the war:

> Constant reflection has made me feel the very high value of
> 'Workshop', provided that a thoroughly good plan can be
> made and it is given a chance. The effect of 'Workshop', if
> successful, would be electrifying, and would greatly increase
> our strategic hold upon the Central Mediterranean. It is also
> a most important step to opening the Narrows to the passage
> of trade and troop convoys, whereby so great an easement to
> our shipping could be obtained . . . [86]

Here is the mature wartime leader at work: urging his generals into
bold action, but not forgetting the need to cover the political flank and
provide 'wriggle-room' in case of disaster. The latter skill was a legacy
of the 'backlash' after the Churchill-advocated Gallipoli campaign in
1915 went wrong – disastrously for the New Zealand and Australian
forces which bore the brunt of the fighting. Churchill's domination
of the decision-making process led to public criticism and his own
resignation after the report of the 'Dardanelles Commission' in 1917.

The great lesson learned by Churchill from this episode was that safety for political leaders in the event of military mishaps could be secured only if the military commanders in the field were on record as active supporters of the decision to proceed.

The date of Churchill's pressing minute, and the destination of T9046 on the night of 12 January, make it reasonable to guess that the Sunderland may have alighted on the African coast near Pantelleria with commandos, the '2 passengers', perhaps to assess enemy strength and the terrain for the operation. The ORB records that 'Aircraft landed by moonlight a few miles out to sea and taxied in to within half-a-mile. Agents were disembarked in a small dinghy towing another containing bicycles. Aircraft then taxied out to sea and took off.' In the event, 'Workshop' never proceeded, being soon eclipsed by the increasingly besieged position of Malta itself.

In January 1941, 228 Squadron had five Sunderlands at Kalafrana Bay with a staple flying diet of ten-hour patrols over the Ionian Sea. The squadron also had at its disposal two unfamilar French aircraft: a Latécoere 298B float-plane and a Loire 130 flying boat. The Latécoere had arrived in Malta on 5 July 1940 when, following the fall of France, two pilots of the Aeronavale at Bizerta in Tunisia, René Duvauchelle and Jacques Melhouas, had resolved to continue the fight by joining the British forces with their machine. The story of their escape to Malta is well told in Frederick Galea's account of wartime operations at Kalafrana Bay.[87] The Loire 130 had been aboard the French battleship *Richelieu*, from which it could be launched by catapult. Its crew, Georges Blaize and Raoul Gatien, diverted to Malta during a flight on 15 October 1940. These two smaller French aircraft were used by 228 Squadron for clandestine operations, and Alec flew both: the Latécoere on 18 February and the Loire on 25 and 31 January, and again on 17 February.

By March 1941, the serious entry of the Luftwaffe to the Mediterranean – in the form of Oberleutnant Joachim Muncheberg and his fighter squadron, 7 Staffel/ Jagdgeschwader 26 – was making Kalafrana Bay, and the alternative mooring at Saint Paul's, very dangerous places for the Sunderlands. Muncheberg was already a German fighter ace, having seen action in the invasion of France, with 23 victories to his credit and a recently awarded Knight's Cross.[88] Now, his unit's Messerschmitt 109Es, with nose cowlings painted bright yellow with a superimposed red heart, ranged from their base at Gela in Sicily to attack Malta, and were very ready to pounce on the targets presented by moored or taxiing flying boats.

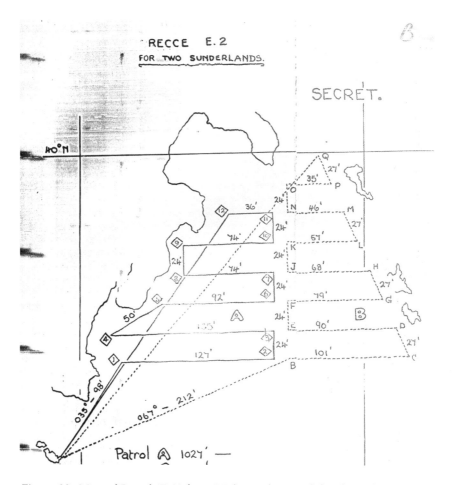

Figure 32: Map of Patrol 'E.2' from Malta (at bottom left) along the coasts of Sicily and Italy and over the Ionian Sea. From 228 Squadron ORB, National Archives, London. Alec flew similar patrols on several occasions.

On 7 March, 228 Squadron's Sunderland L2164 was strafed at its moorings in Saint Paul's Bay. Sergeant A.S. Jones, boatguard on the flying boat, was killed while engaging the German fighters with the gas-operated Vickers gun from the mid-ships gun port. Twenty-two years old, from Aberaryon in west Wales, Alan Jones stood no chance against the 20 mm cannon fire of the Messerschmitts at point-blank range. It was a reminder that the dangers of flying-boat operations were shared by all squadron members.

Three days later, on 10 March, the German fighters were back:

A low flying machine gun attack was made by a formation
of Me 109s – they directed their fire at T9046 which was
damaged, and then on L2164 which caught fire . . . the machine
was towed ashore & beached but had to be abandoned and
ultimately sank. Although a number of personnel had narrow
escapes there were no casualties.[89]

Alec's entry in the logbook was laconic: 'shot up by 109's at St Pauls
on water'.

In April 2005 I sat on rocks above the entrance to the little
Mistra Bay at Saint Paul's, where Sunderlands L2164 and T9046
were strafed, and thought about the ascendancy of the German
pilots in 1941. The German air force was the hammer of Hitler's
strategy in the Western Mediterranean, and soon in Greece and
Crete as well. However, and unsuspected by the German command,
it was simultaneously poisoning Hitler's fortunes in the Middle
East. The deciphering of the Luftwaffe's 'Enigma' communications
in 1940–41 gave British intelligence its best information on German
movements, intentions, weaknesses, and assessments in the theatre.
Not only did 'reading' the air force's Enigma radio traffic provide

Figure 33: The entrance to Mistra Bay in Saint Paul's Bay, Malta, April 2005.
Fishing boats are moored now where Sunderlands L2164 and T9046 rode in 1941.
Sergeant Alan Jones was killed here on 7 March 1941 while engaging attacking
fighters at close range. L2164 later sank nearby.

a direct window into Luftwaffe planning and movements, but also, as the air force relayed information received from army and navy sources to its own units for co-ordination purposes, it indirectly illuminated those matters also, thereby to a significant extent filling the gap left by Bletchley Park's inability to read the German army's Enigma communications until 1942.[90]

Figure 34: Muncheberg descends in triumph from his Me 109E in Sicily, 1941.

It is not necessary to be a military genius to appreciate the enormous advantage enjoyed in war by a commander who is able to read his enemy's most secret communications about the dispositions and intentions of its forces. That advantage is increased in proportion to the enemy's confidence that its coded signals are secure. The great success of the 'Ultra' intelligence provided by Bletchley Park was founded not only on the technical and imaginative brilliance of the British code-breaking teams, but equally on the successful preservation of German confidence in the security of its Enigma communications system, notwithstanding repeated military setbacks caused directly by the British ability to 'read' it.

It may therefore be no coincidence that, after the interception and destruction by Admiral Cunningham of important elements of the Italian fleet off Cape Matapan on 27–28 February 1941, the Luftwaffe began to target the Sunderland flying boats in Malta.

Although we now know that the intelligence on which that action was based came initially from Bletchley Park's decoding of Italian Enigma signals, it was a strict rule that 'Ultra' knowledge could be used only where a plausible alternative source for the information could be inferred. It is a tribute to the role of the Sunderlands in providing both genuine and 'cover' intelligence that the German commanders began to give priority to suppression of the insistent snooping activities of the Malta-based Sunderlands.[91]

On 27 April, Muncheberg himself attacked L5807 in Kalafrana Bay on its return from escorting into Malta Hurricanes flown off the aircraft-carrier *Ark Royal*. The Sunderland burned and sank. Three photographs of the burning flying boat were in my father's papers – the aircraft had a particular significance for him as he had flown the delivery flight from Short's Rochester works to Pembroke Dock for 210 Squadron back in August 1939, and had received night-flying training in it from Wing Commander Nicholetts in January 1941.

Figure 35: Sequence of Sunderland L5807 burning and sinking in Kalafrana Bay,

But already, in March, the predations of Muncheberg's Me 109s over Malta had grown too severe for 228 Squadron's big and slow flying boats – they were vulnerable on reconnaissance flights and at their moorings in Kalafrana Bay and Saint Paul's. The decision was made to move the permanent base eastwards to Alexandria in Egypt, and T9046 flew there on 19 March, joining 230 Squadron, the two units together being designated 201 Group.[92]

Alexandria was founded in 331 BC by the great Alexander at the age of 25. He was in Egypt to further his Persian campaign, and hurried on. When he died eight years later, his body was brought to Memphis (now Cairo) for burial. This was refused by the high priest there, who prophesied that the city of Alexander's burial would be 'uneasy, disturbed with wars and battles'. So it was that the body travelled north to Alexandria to be buried at its great crossroads.

Figure 36: Sunderland undergoing maintenance at Alexandria. The technique for on-the-water engine change is displayed, as is that for cleaning the cockpit canopy. *Imperial War Museum CM2457.*

E.M. Forster's classic *Alexandria: A History and a Guide*, first published in 1922, traces the devolution of the city to one of Alexander's generals, Ptolemy, who founded the dynasty of that name. One of its figures, Ptolemy Soter, created the great Mouseion library at Alexandria and a tradition of learning and scholarship which brought the sciences of mathematics, geography, astronomy, and medicine to new heights. The authority of the new scholarship is suggested by Euclid's curt remark to Ptolemy Philadelphus, who, thinking that his exalted status might bring accelerated understanding, was informed that there was 'no royal road to geometry'.

In 1941, the harbour at Alexandria was crowded with warships and transports, in addition to the maritime commerce which had made the ancient city a hub of Mediterranean trade. It was also subject to air attacks at night. Lawrence Durrell has his character Darley in *Clea* arrive as a refugee from Greece in April 1941 during such a raid:

> . . . the nearer distance glowed pink as a sea-shell, deepening gradually into the rose-richness of a flower. A faint and terrible moaning came out across the water towards us, pulsing like the wing-beats of some fearful prehistoric bird . . . A dense stream of coloured rockets now began to mount from the haze among the battleships, emptying on the sky their brilliant clusters of stars and diamonds and smashed pearl snuff-boxes with marvellous prodigality . . . [93]

Flying boats found the harbour hazardous for taxiing. In November 1940, 230 Squadron's L5804 hit a native felucca

> . . . which had been obscured from pilot's view. Speed of a/c [aircraft] was such as to make avoiding action impossible. Pilot not to blame. Native in charge of felucca failed to obey warning. Blue Pennant flown from HM ships when a/c TO or lands.[94]

The investigation concluded that the accident was the result of 'the congested state of the harbour' and the confused control of the port by the civil authorities, the Royal Navy, and the RAF. Strangely, the same aircraft struck another felucca some months later.

In June 1941 Sunderland T9071 of the Australian No 10 Squadron hit a tanker while taxiing to take off for the UK: 'Harbour was congested and there is little room for T.O.'s [take-offs] in upwind direction about N.W . . . No blame on pilot.'[95]

To ease the pressure, the main operational base was moved to Aboukir Bay, 15 miles eastwards along the Corniche from Alexandria. Henry Lamond remembers that the living arrangements in Alexandria were difficult, with 228 Squadron's airmen being billeted in 'boat houses' which were full of bed-bugs. 'We preferred to sleep on the floor rather than endure the insects in the bedding,' Henry told me.

In May 2003 my accommodation at the Plaza Hotel on Alexandria's Corniche was more salubrious. I had with me wartime photos of a Sunderland taking off with a water tower in the background. I guessed that the scene was Aboukir Bay,

Figure 37: Sunderland taking off at Aboukir Bay, near Alexandria, with Fort Ramleh water-tower in background. *Imperial War Museum CM2317.*

but wanted to check this, and to get the feel of the historic spot near the ancient and now dried-up 'Canopic' mouth of the Nile. Here, in 1798, Nelson destroyed Napoleon's fleet under Admiral Brueys in what is sometimes called the 'Battle of the Nile'. In recent years, the French marine archaeologist Franck Goddio has been not only uncovering wrecks from the battle but also making amazing discoveries in the same area from the ancient and now underwater city of Heracleion, which seems to have served as a trading port as early as the sixth century BC and into the times of Greek domination. The city and its huge temple of Amun appear to have been submerged following earthquakes and tidal waves in the first century BC.

I was picked up at 9 am by my driver and guide for the day, Omar Mohamed, a pleasant and careful young man with just enough English to make basic communication possible, to whom I explained the purpose of my visit. We drove eastwards along the Corniche towards the village of Aboukir. As we passed through the heavy traffic along the beaches on the Mediterranean shore, I thought of Evelyn Waugh's descriptions of Alexandria in 1941:

Guy went to the car-park and found a lorry going in for rations. The road ran along the edge of the sea. The breeze was full of flying sand. On the beaches young civilians exposed hairy bodies and played ball with loud, excited cries. Army lorries passed in close procession, broken here and there by new, tight-shut limousines bearing purple-lipped ladies in black satin. [96]

Figure 38: 'Mando' the boatman (left) and Omar the driver in Aboukir Bay during the author's visit in 2003.

At Aboukir, it became apparent that the security areas around the Egyptian naval base would be a problem. Our way seemed blocked. Omar drove to the point at the western end of the bay and went into a fish restaurant named Zephyrion. His inquiries there led us to a nearby fishing village and a complicated negotiation on the shore with the owner of a bright yellow, canvas-canopied fishing boat. Soon, we boarded the boat and the owner's son, Mando, started the motor and had us on our way seawards. A mile or two out, I spread my pictures of Sunderlands on the engine cover – a picture is worth a thousand words! Mando grinned in recognition and pointed back at the shore where the waterworks at Fort Ramleh were unmistakably those visible in the pictures.

We chugged our way towards Nelson's Island, perhaps two miles off shore. I thought of the seamanship of Nelson and his captains, which got English men-o'-war on the inside of Admiral Brueys's ships on 1 August 1798 – just about where we were. Forster's delightful book on Alexandria summarises the result:

> The engagement began at 6.0 pm. At 7.0 Brueys was killed, at 9.30 the *Orient* (the French flagship) caught fire and blew up shortly afterwards; the explosion was tremendous and terminated the first act of the battle; an interval of appalled silence followed . . . The fighting recommenced and, continuing through the night, and ending at midday on the 2nd with the complete victory of Nelson. The French fleet had been annihilated; only two Men-of-War and two Frigates escaped, and Napoleon had lost for ever his command of the Mediterranean . . . [97]

I pulled a camera from my rucksack and took a picture of Nelson's Island. Omar and Mando looked nervous. 'No photo', said Omar urgently, pointing towards the Egyptian warships and naval installations on the shore. I put my camera away and my companions resumed their cheerful moods as we completed an arc through Aboukir Bay.

That night I returned to Aboukir, having decided that the Zephyrion restaurant looked too interesting to miss. As I entered the brightly lit stucco doorway, a large proprietorial man loomed energetically before me gesticulating and shouting – 'Jews, Jews', he seemed to say. I wondered whether this was my first taste of anti-Western sentiment as the American air war in Iraq continued. No, 'Choose, choose' was the instruction. I was being directed to the kitchen and its large water-filled pots containing live fish, crustaceans, and shellfish, to make my selection for dinner. I was duly served an excellent meal of prawns and a grilled sea bass. A card on my table told me that the restaurant was established in 1929, and the proprietor was named Periclis N. Tsaparis. I had read somewhere that the fishing industry at Aboukir had for centuries been in the hands of a Sicilian community. I guessed that the Zephyrion was part of it – and that the Sunderland pilots in 1941 would have had many a meal in this proudly run restaurant overlooking the little beach at the point.

Lawrence Durrell was in Alexandria in 1941 and wrote of the wartime city:

... a place for dramatic partings, irrevocable decisions, last thoughts; everyone feels pushed to the extreme, to the end of his bent ... The city does nothing. You hear nothing but the noise of the sea and the echoes of an extraordinary history.[98]

'Eunostos' was the ancient name of Alexandria harbour itself, and Durrell says that, in 1941, 'To many of our sailors it was still Eunostos, "port of safe return", as it had been in Homer's time.'

Few details of 228 Squadron's 'off duty' activities in Alexandria are available. The squadron ORB records that, on 3 May 1941, 'The whole Squadron went into Alexandria to see their late Commanding Officer Wing Commander Nicholetts off to his new posting.' Henry Lamond's younger brother, another Alec, then serving with the New Zealand forces in Cairo, told me in 2003 that he travelled to Alexandria in 1941 to meet Henry, finding him at a golf course, playing a round with my father.

On 22 February 1941 Lieutenant Colonel Robert Lees, the 'Adviser in Venereology – Middle East', reported on the sexual temptations and dangers to which British and Commonwealth forces in Egypt were exposed in Cairo and Alexandria. Lees concluded that 'There is no doubt that the forces are surrounded by an alien population with extremely low moral standards'.[99] The report cited figures: in the three months up to December 1940, 574 cases of venereal disease had been reported to police in Alexandria. More than 800 women had been arrested for soliciting, and 150 clandestine brothels had been closed. In Alexandria 27,860 servicemen had used the 'prophylactic ablution centre', and 32,000 in Cairo.

Lawrence Durrell, writing to Henry Miller in 1944, gives part of the explanation for the outbreak of sexual activity:

Alexandria is, after Hollywood, fuller of beautiful women than any place else. Incomparably more beautiful than Athens or Paris; the mixture Coptic, Jewish, Syrian, Egyptian, Moroccan, Spanish, gives you slant eyes, olive freckled skin, hawk-lips and noses, and a temperament like a bomb. Sexual provender of quality but the atmosphere is damp, hysterical, sandy, with the wind off the desert fanning everything to mania.[100]

General Wavell's Middle East headquarters were in Cairo, and the Sunderlands of 228 and 230 Squadrons visited the city when needed

to ferry 'top brass' to Mediterranean destinations. Artemis Cooper
has provided a vivid picture of wartime Cairo:

> The bobbing line of turbans and tarbooshes that threaded
> its way along the pavements was speckled by khaki caps in
> a variety of styles, but the city was still pervaded with the
> familiar smell of the urban Middle East: a blend of exhaust
> fumes, over-worked pack animals, cheap incense, and manure
> ... Groppi's, the most famous café in Cairo, was fragrant
> with the smell of roasting coffee and fresh pastry cooked in
> clarified butter. In Shepheard's Hotel, the stocks of decent
> Hock and Champagne did not run out until 1943.[101]

In 1941 the hulls of the Sunderlands planed over the historical layers
of Aboukir Bay, the legacies of the Pharaohs, and of Bonaparte and
Nelson, as they came and went on their missions to Malta, Greece,
and Crete. Soon they would add to those layers. At least two
Sunderlands of 230 Squadron are recorded as having crashed and
sunk in Aboukir Bay: T9050 on 30 September 1941, and W3987[102]
on 7 September 1942.

6. Greece – Getting in and Getting out

In May 2003 I left my hotel just off Syntagma Square in Athens, near the elegantly refurbished Hotel Grande Bretagne, which in 1941 had successively accommodated the leading British and then German generals, and made my way to the bus station for the three-hour journey to Nauplion in the Bay of Argos. Soon, the efficient and reasonably priced KTEL bus was heading out of Athens towards Lake Eleusis. Here, in 1941, was the flying-boat base of Scaramanga, which served as a forward base for the Sunderlands of 228 and 230 Squadrons. The crews relished the climate there:

> Our shore installations were a partly completed Greek Torpedo Depot at Scaramanga, lying at the foot of Mount Daphne . . . A most impressive feature . . . was the marvellous feeling of well-being on breathing the cool, scented airs descending from those pine-clad mountains; such a contrast from the sandy heat of Egypt and Malta.[103]

My bus ran along the now heavily industrialised shore, with its Asian car manufacturing, and dozens of ships rode in the bay gleaming in the May sun through the *nefos* or smog. Soon, we could see the island of Salamis, where Themistocles and his Athenian squadrons destroyed the Persian fleet of Xerxes in 480 BC.

Plutarch tells us that, at daybreak on the day of that battle, Xerxes had a golden throne set up at the point where Salamis is separated from the mainland by only a narrow channel – there, Plutarch says, the king and his secretaries prepared to record the events. On the Athenian side, Themistocles, reluctantly we are told, followed the advice of his prophet to sacrifice to Dionysus three young prisoners dressed in gold ornaments.

Aeschylus asserts that Xerxes had a thousand ships and Plutarch reckons the Athenian contingent at 180 triremes with 18 fighters on each deck. The manoeuvrability of these smaller and lower Athenian vessels proved decisive, however, as the high-decked and larger Persian ships broached in the sea swell and fouled one

another. Byron's lines remind us of the stark finality of defeat in
large set-piece battle:[104]

> A king sate on the rocky brow
> Which looks o'er sea-born Salamis;
> And ships, by thousands, lay below,
> And men in nations; – all were his!
> He counted them at break of day –
> And when the sun set where were they?

Such was the fame and mystique gained by Themistocles from the
great victory at Salamis that, Plutarch says, when he entered the
stadium at the next Olympic games, 'The audience took no further
interest in the competitors, but spent the whole day gazing at him,
pointing him out to strangers and admiring and applauding him
as they did so.' Comparable stakes and reputations now hung on
decisions to be made by General Sir Archibald Wavell, the overall
commander of British forces in the Middle East, as he considered his
position in the Middle East and Mediterranean in 1941.

On 10 April 1941, T9046 took off from Aboukir Bay and made
the short flight south to Cairo to prepare for an important mission.
The logbook shows that Alec was accompanied on the flight deck
by the Rhodesia-trained Pilot Officer Paré and Sergeant Massam. At
dawn on 11 April, Good Friday, the Sunderland took off from Cairo
on a 'cold and dull morning'. Aboard were some very distinguished
passengers: General Wavell and Air Chief Marshal Longmore,
together with fifteen staff. The destination was Athens.

We have earlier had a glimpse of Arthur Longmore at Calshot in
1929 when, along with the Rector of Waitaki Boys' High School,
Frank Milner, and nearly a million other spectators, he watched the
Schneider Trophy Race. This remarkable Australian-born sailor-
turned-aviator had been plucked from his torpedo-boat in 1910 to
learn to fly under Horace Short himself. After two and a half hours
of tuition he flew solo in 1911 and became one of the founding
instructors of the British flying-boat tradition. At Cromarty in
northern Scotland in 1913 he took the young First Lord of the
Admiralty, Winston Churchill, up in his Borel seaplane:

> I can well recollect our flight in the Borel: it was one of
> those perfect autumn evenings and from 5000 feet we had
> the most beautiful view right across the hills and mountains
> of Scotland with their wonderful colour effects. We both

enjoyed it immensely. Winston was anxious to know what
we young enthusiasts thought about how the development of
flying would affect naval warfare.[105]

In 1914, Longmore demonstrated the feasibility of dropping a
torpedo from an aeroplane. Now, he commanded the RAF's
resources in the Middle East. Relations with his former passenger,
Winston Churchill, were deteriorating in the crucible of military
reverse.

Among the fifteen passengers accompanying Wavell and
Longmore at the dawn boarding of T9046 in Cairo on 11 April
was a staff officer from Cairo headquarters, Francis de Guignand,
whose account provided the weather report mentioned earlier:

> I was waiting for the launch to take me off, when I sensed a
> certain amount of excitement behind me, and looking round
> was rather shaken to see Wavell getting out of his car. I did
> my best to fade into the background, but he had spotted me
> and called out, 'De Guignand, what are you doing here?' I
> walked over, feeling rather like a small boy who had been
> caught stealing apples in a neighbour's orchard . . . [106]

De Guignand's discomfort arose from Wavell's supposed disapproval
of his planning for a possible evacuation of Greece even before the
British-led expeditionary force had arrived in Athens. De Guignand
continued his narrative:

> When my turn came to go aboard, I crept in rather like a
> fugitive and made for the tail of the machine, where I found
> somewhere to sit away from the V.I.P.'s cabin. When I judged
> that we were somewhere near Crete, I decided that I must have
> a peep at this great island which was to be used as a stepping-
> stone in our evacuation plans. The crew allowed me into the
> observation deck, and it was not long before the western end
> of Crete was visible far below, looking beautiful and serene
> with the unbelievable blue waters of the Mediterranean
> lapping its shores . . .

Flight Lieutenant Frame's Sunderland T9046 on its six-hour flight
to Athens had become the temporary headquarters for some very
anxious commanders. This Friday was not particularly 'good'
for Wavell, now a tired and hard-pressed general. From 6 April
it was clear that Rommel had swept all before him in his drive

eastwards along the North African coast and that British resistance was crumbling. Three of Wavell's generals had been overrun and captured. The decision to divert forces from North Africa to Greece, to be discussed in Chapter 7, now looked unfortunate, to say the least. The British Foreign Secretary, Anthony Eden, recalled Wavell's jest when he and the Chief of the Imperial General Staff, Sir John Dill, left Cairo for London on 7 April: 'He came out in the launch to our flying boat, and as we were about to get on board remarked to the C.I.G.S. "I hope, Jack, that you will preside over my court-martial".'[107]

Only three days before T9046's flight to Greece, on 8 April, Wavell had flown by Lockheed Hudson west to Tobruk to prepare the defence there. On attempting to return to Cairo, the aircraft made a forced landing in the desert, leaving the general stumbling about in the dark for many hours. Meanwhile, Churchill's messages, often couched in biting language, were demanding offensive action in Iraq and Syria. Wavell had dusted off his 'worst case scenario' file, contemplating the possible loss of Egypt altogether and some kind of regrouping in southern Africa. His military biographer, General R.J. Collins, summarised his predicament and his condition:

> The combination of both mental and physical strain – the former quite as wearing as the latter – was beginning to tell even on his iron nerve and frame. He was carrying in his head – in some detail – five separate campaigns, Abyssinia, Eritrea, Iraq, Cyrenaica, and Greece. In each of these his was the controlling if not the directing brain . . . Over and above this, too, there was the moral strain. Only those who have been in a responsible position in battle have the faintest idea of how great this strain can be. It is greatest naturally in a retreat or when things are going badly . . . He is the target for all eyes. From his words his subordinate commanders . . . all strive to learn how the battle is going: what the chances are: whether disaster or victory, or at least safety, lies ahead.[108]

The twin movements – British forces to Greece and German forces to north Africa – were well described by a contemporary official account:

> The Germans seized the moment to send a powerful armoured force to the assistance of the Italians in Tripolitania. This force was indeed more powerful than that which we were

sending to Greece. The situation at the end of March was therefore rather like that of two men passing each other through a revolving door. While we pushed into Europe, the Germans pushed into Africa.[109]

The British explorer and adventurer Freya Stark, then staying at the British Embassy in Cairo, and a friend and admirer of Wavell, noticed that the general's usual equanimity became disturbed at this time:

> General Wilson and Lord Wavell are the only two commanders I have known, so to say, in action, and both have given the impression of calmness and efficient leisure – the quiet which is said to be in the heart of the tornado . . . Only once did I see him [Wavell] deflected by the thought of trouble. It was at a wedding in the spring of 1941, when he gave away the bride in the absence of her father.[110]

Wavell was a man of letters, the biographer of General Allenby, under whom he had served in World War I.[111] In his preface explaining the decision to publish a portion of this unfinished work, Wavell wrote from Middle East headquarters in June 1940 that the war had interrupted the writing, adding with masterly understatement that 'there is little prospect of my having time to write the remaining chapters at present'. On the page opposite, Wavell quotes Socrates' summary of the desired attributes of a general:

> The general must know how to get his men their rations and every other kind of stores needed in war. He must have imagination to originate plans, practical sense and energy to carry them through. He must be observant, untiring, shrewd, kindly and cruel, simple and crafty, a watchman and a robber, lavish and miserly, generous and stingy, rash and conservative. All these and many other qualities, natural and acquired, he must have. He should also, as a matter of course, know his tactics; for a disorderly mob is no more an army than a heap of building materials is a house.

Wavell's assessment of Allenby, whose military reputation rested on his triumphant Palestinian campaigns in 1917–18, tells us something of Wavell's own approach to high military command. As to the decision to break off the drive towards Tripoli in favour of the expedition to Greece, he must surely have reminded himself of one of

Allenby's favourite maxims: 'Once you have taken a decision, never look back on it'. On the other hand, he might also have ruefully pondered his own recent abandonment of pursuit of the fleeing Italian forces in Libya in the context of this judgement on Allenby: 'As a general in high command he used surprise and mobility as his main weapons . . . these, and relentless vigour in pursuit, are the principal lessons that students of his campaigns will note.'[112]

Of Wavell's reading on the long flights around his command in 1941 we know a little: *Alice in Wonderland* on his way back from Athens to Cairo in mid-March, and *Anthony and Cleopatra* a month later on the same route as he hedge-hopped away from a burning Athens airfield with his army in full retreat.[113] Although Anthony's amorous distraction had no parallel in Wavell's predicament, there was military disaster to share, and the finger-pointing of 'our slippery people, whose love is never linked to the deserver till his deserts are past . . . '[114]

Another snapshot of Wavell comes from Evelyn Waugh's *Officers and Gentlemen*, where we see the general at a dinner party. Waugh captures both the soldier's anguish and his love of scholarship and the arts in this passage:

> The Commander-in Chief was despondent as he had good reason to be. Everything was out of his control and everything was going wrong. He ate in silence. At length he said:
> 'I'll tell you the best poem written in Alexandria.'
> 'Recitation,' said Mrs Stitch.
> 'They told me, Heraclitus, they told me you were dead
>   . . . '[115]

The full poem by Callimachus, singing of the immortality of artistic achievement, is quoted by Forster in his book on Alexandria:

> Someone told me, Heraclitus, of your end;
> and I wept, and thought how often you and I
> sunk the sun with talking. Well! and now
> you lie antiquated ashes somewhere, Carian friend.
> But your nightingales, your songs, are living still;
> Them the death that clutches all things cannot kill.[116]

Behind these literary diversions, the British army command structure in the theatre was as follows: Wavell in overall command in the Mediterranean; 'Jumbo' Wilson in command in Greece; Generals Blamey and Mackay having special responsibilities for Australian troops; and General Freyberg similarly placed in relation to New Zealand troops. On Good Friday 1941, a weary Wavell, an anxious Longmore, and the uncomfortable de Guignand, were arriving in Athens aboard Sunderland T9046, as the last relates:

> Finally, we came within sight of Athens and the great port of Piraeus and, after circling round, made a perfect landing on the smooth water; we then taxied to a mooring buoy, a launch came alongside and Wavell and his party left for the landing stage . . .

Alec's logbook is clear that the alighting was at Scaramanga. Further, the devastation of Piraeus on 6 April by German bombing and the catastrophic explosion of an ammunition ship there make that port a highly unlikely place of arrival. The Sunderlands seem to have been a welcome and reassuring sight in the skies over Athens at this time. One newspaper reported that 'a giant war-scarred British Sunderland flying boat circled over the Acropolis and roared low over Athens – a symbol of a promise that has now passed beyond the stage of words'.[117]

The reputations of fighting generals are fragile. All make mistakes of one kind or other at one time or another, and the verdict of history seems to hang on how the balance of advantage is reckoned when the successes are tabled against the failures by the historians of the future. A general will have made both friends and enemies – that's just on his *own* side – in the course of a military career. His friends can be relied on to 'make the case' for posterity in his favour, sometimes too uncritically and enthusiastically for his own good. His enemies, however, will lose no chance to minimise victories, or attribute them to the work of others. As for reverses, they will emphatically be sheeted home to the failures of the unfortunate commander, around whom constructions of the 'if only he had . . . ' kind will be erected with perfect hindsight. The relationship between a general and the political leadership of the state is also a vital factor. When purely military considerations are affected by political judgements, even wise ones, the task of the general becomes most perilous.

In his 1964 book *Generals at War*, Sir Francis de Guignand challenged the 'legend' of Wavell as set out in General Collins's study. His main criticism was that Wavell failed to stand up to Churchill's advocacy of the expedition to Greece, known as 'Operation LUSTRE'. De Guignand claimed that Wavell knew, or should have known, that the mission was militarily impossible and could end only in evacuation, and should have told Churchill so, and offered his resignation if the Prime Minister continued to insist on its pursuit. De Guignand avowed:

> I now hold the very definite conviction that the main blame must be placed upon Wavell because he failed to stand up to political pressure when he should have done ... It was virtually against Wavell's orders, and in spite of his opposition, that the vital studies and preparations for the inevitable move out of Greece were available when required.[118]

Churchill's defence of the expedition to Greece was that it served higher state interests to which even strategic military calculations had to defer. First, the credibility of the state was at stake: how would it seem to present and potential future allies if undertakings of support were abandoned? Second, Churchill stressed the usefulness of the 'valiant defence of Greek democracy' in strengthening President Roosevelt's resolve to break free of the constraints of the Neutrality Acts in order to supply war *matériel* to the beleaguered British forces in the Middle East and other theatres.

The background to, and soundness of, this 'higher purpose' argument will be examined in Chapter 7, dealing with the pressures for and against American involvement in the conflict, but for the moment it is enough to say that the political context of the decision was well understood by contemporary observers. For example, Sir John White, General Freyberg's personal assistant at the time, gave this New Zealand perspective:

> The real reason behind the decision to send an expeditionary force to Greece will no doubt be revealed by historians with access to all the archives. Considered immediately after the event it seemed clear that the adventure must have been known to be almost hopeless from the start. Why then was it undertaken at a time when more disasters and more loss of equipment were highly dangerous? History will show no doubt that the reasons were political and moral; it was important that Great Britain should give the gallant Greek Nation what support she could. It was important that the United States, not yet in the war, should see that the British were going to fight. And New Zealand's Prime Minister, Mr Fraser, must have been thinking of these things when he

said in Parliament after the campaign was over that if the New Zealand Government had to decide again whether to allow the New Zealand Division to go to Greece, the decision would be the same.[119]

The political dimension of the decision to go to Greece is evident in the records of the key meetings in London. At the Defence Committee meeting on 8 January 1941, Churchill is recorded as saying, no doubt with his record of pre-war anti-appeasement in mind, that the Greeks 'would be likely to see whether yet again one of our friends was to be trampled down without our being able to prevent their fate'. The meeting agreed that 'It was of the first importance, *from the political point of view*, that we should do everything possible, *by hook or by crook*, to send at once to Greece the fullest support within our power.'[120]

The key paper, dated 24 February 1941, prepared by the Chiefs of Staff for the War Cabinet, bore even more explicitly the imprint of the Churchill-driven political imperative, and also drew on earlier meetings at Cairo between Eden, Dill, Wavell, Longmore, and Cunningham, which will receive more attention in Chapter 7. The service chiefs began by observing:

> It goes without saying that the operation must be a gamble, but our representatives on the spot . . . evidently think that there is a reasonable prospect of successfully holding up a German advance. We feel that we must accept their opinion.

The paper went on to tabulate a 'balance sheet' of advantage and disadvantage, and came in paragraph 6 to 'Political Considerations':

> Politically it seems to us that there would be serious disadvantages if we were to fail to help Greece. The effect on public opinion throughout the world, *particularly in America*, of our deserting a small nation which is already engaged in a magnificent fight against one oppressor and is willing to defy another, would be lamentable.

The paper's conclusion is a confession of the ascendancy of political over military calculation: 'the risks of failure are serious . . . Even the complete failure of an honourable attempt to help Greece need not be disastrous to our future ability to defeat Germany.'[121]

The answer to de Guignand's criticisms may be that Wavell

accepted the political necessity for the expedition to Greece, and loyally followed the directions of his political master, as he was constitutionally bound to do. Yet Wavell cannot escape a suggestion that he dealt with the Australian and New Zealand hesitations by telling Blamey and Freyberg that their governments had approved the plan, while telling the two governments that Blamey and Freyberg had expressed support for it. An ancient stratagem.

Another explanation for Wavell's willingness to accommodate Churchill's political need to go to Greece has been offered by Robin Higham, who suggests that Wavell had calculated that the German offensive in Greece would be so well advanced by the time the British force arrived, and the Greek army so near the point of inevitable surrender, that Wavell's force could decently have been diverted or withdrawn before serious engagement. Higham suggests that it was the delay in the German attack, caused by bad weather, which upset that timetable and left Wavell's expedition more deeply engaged than expected:

> If all had gone according to the usual German schedule, if the snows had melted in time in the Bulgarian passes, the Germans should have been well past the Aliakmon line before the British had even begun to get into position . . . The people who did not understand the realities were in London. They were the ones whom Wavell had to deceive. Thus OPERATION LUSTRE evolved. It was designed to satisfy Churchill with a show of force, to be a gesture to a gallant ally that would not cost the British and Commonwealth forces too much.[122]

De Guignand had begun a planning paper for evacuation even before the expeditionary force arrived in Greece, and claims that Wavell tried to stop this work. The truth may have been that Wavell knew that evacuation was probably the end-game in Greece, and that planning had to be done for it. His ambivalent attitude to the planners arose out of the need to compartmentalise his thinking between military and political approaches. No commander can admit to his front-line lieutenants that the battle is lost before it has started. It may be also that planning for evacuation was an unwelcome reminder that the adventure in Greece was a military sacrifice with political objectives.

On the day after the arrival in Athens aboard Sunderland T9046, de Guignand was surprised to receive a telephone call from Wavell asking to meet him at the Hotel Grand Bretagne that afternoon. He relates that Wavell greeted him with, 'Oh, there you are, Freddie', proceeded to paint a bleak picture of the military situation, and declared that 'it now looks as if we shall have to consider evacuation'.

De Guignand was particularly incensed by what he took to be a suggestion in Collins's account that Wavell had evacuations plans in hand at all relevant stages, pointing particularly to these passages in Collins:

> Wavell's second visit to Greece had brought home to him the immense difficulties . . . It was for this reason, that as soon as he got back to Cairo . . . he instructed the Joint Planning Staff to prepare secretly a plan for the evacuation . . .

> Wavell was forced to return to Greece, where affairs had reached such a critical stage . . . [he] had, of course, realized for some days that he might be faced with this terrible problem and had done all he could to prepare for it . . . He took with him a small staff which had been studying the problems and which had skeleton plans already in hand . . . [123]

But I think we may untangle this dispute. The first passage refers to Wavell's visit in T9046 on 11 April, while the second refers to a *further and different* visit by the general on 19 April. So read, the account is surely unexceptionable: on the 11th Wavell gives de Guignand and his fellow planners the green light, on the 19th he is entitled to claim that 'he had . . . realized for some days . . . and done all he could to prepare for it'. The suggestion that Collins has distorted the record so as to attribute to Wavell greater prescience, or less negligence, falls away when the references are so understood.

Wavell's journey to Greece in T9046 on Good Friday had as its main purpose an on-the-ground assessment of the military situation. We have earlier seen that it resulted in the general's conclusion that evacuation would be necessary. More immediately, orders were given on the night of 11 April for withdrawal to a new defensive line running from Mount Olympus in the east along the River Aliakmon. Another decision taken with the commanders of the New Zealand and Australian forces, Freyberg and Blamey, was to rename the New Zealand Division and the 6th Australian Division the ANZAC Corps, 'reviving for a new generation the memory of their predecessors' greatness'.[124]

Figure 39: General Freyberg, apparently amused after the strafing of his staff car during the pull-back in Greece, April 1941. Brigadier K.L. Stewart with dark glasses at rear. *Collection of J.C. White.*

The return flight of T9046 to Egypt on 13 April had its own problems. During the night of the 12th German aircraft had dropped mines in the harbour off Scaramanga. The ORB explains the technique used to ensure a safe take-off: 'The captain of the aircraft Fl. Lt. Frame was shown the areas in which it was believed the mines had landed. The take off was made on the path made in taxiing.' We may assume that the distinguished passengers were not boarded until the path had been thus tested. Air Marshal Longmore mused: 'We speculated on the effect of a metal flying-boat passing over a magnetic mine at high speed during the take-off, but nothing happened.'[125]

As Wavell grappled with his military difficulties in Athens on 12 April, Churchill cultivated American sympathy at home. Churchill's secretary, John Colville, reported in his diary for that day on the Prime Minister's tour of south-west England with American Ambassador John G. Winant and Averell Harriman. In Bristol, the party

... walked and motored through devastation such as I had
never thought possible ... There had been a bad raid during
the night and many of the ruins were still smoking. The
people looked bewildered but, as at Swansea, were brave and
were thrilled by the sight of Winston who drove about sitting
on the hood of an open car and waving his hat.[126]

That evening, back at Chequers, the British Prime Minister's country
house, the party received important news from Washington. It was
Roosevelt's telegram announcing the plan for American forces to
patrol the Atlantic. On 13 April Churchill told Roosevelt: 'Deeply
grateful for your momentous cable [of 11 April] just handed me by
Ambassador Winant. Will cable tomorrow at greater length, but
have no doubt that 25th Meridian is a long step towards salvation
... '[127]

Wavell and Longmore, aboard T9046 flying back to Egypt,
absorbed this good news and its implications for their future supply.
But on the same day events forced Churchill to discuss with the
War Cabinet the possibility of a complete collapse of the British
position in Egypt in the face of Rommel's apparently unstoppable
drive eastwards towards Cairo.[128]

By 16 April, Churchill had seen the writing on the wall for Greece,
and instructed Wavell: 'We cannot remain in Greece against wish of
Greek Commander-in-Chief and thus expose country to devastation
... evacuation should proceed ... '[129]

The Prime Minister's displeasure with Wavell was now open, with
his complaint on 18 April about the lack of reporting to London on
the course of fighting in Greece: 'This is not the way His Majesty's
Government should be treated ... I wish you to make sure that this
state of things ends at once ... '[130]

The inevitability of withdrawal from Greece having been
accepted, Wavell's return to Cairo was followed by the appointment
of senior officers from each service to co-ordinate the evacuation.
The bail-out team was led by two able officers, Admiral H.T. Baillie-
Grohman ('B.G')[131] and Group Captain Pelly, who at 9.30 am on 17
April boarded T9046 in Cairo for a daylight flight to Scaramanga.
Unusually, the logbook does not list the passengers, but the 228
Squadron ORB records them as being aboard along with '12 army
and navy officers'. The logbook may be forgiven its preoccupation
with another matter on this occasion: the loss of the port-inner
Pegasus engine in flight.

A good picture of how the ordinary soldier saw the calamities on the ground in Greece in April 1941 emerges from the diary of Sergeant J.W.G. Pickett of the New Zealand Artillery. The sparse, scrawled entries in a tiny pocket-book[132] tell the story:

> *Friday 11 April* – Good Friday. In the pass. Cold – rain – wind
> *Saturday 12 April* – Hail & Sleet. Rain – snow.
> *Sunday 13 April* – Snow. Cold
> *Tuesday 15 April* – left pass about 6 pm for Thermopylae
> *Thursday 17 April* – Rained like I've never see before. Wet through. – on guns all night
> *Sunday 20 April* – Pulled out in a big hurry – just one jump ahead of the Hun
> *Monday 21 April* – Got to within 10 miles of Larissa – bombed – 6 right across in a line. Paced out distance to nearest bomb. 16 paces. Left Larissa 6.30 pm. Parachutists landing.
> *Tuesday 22 April* – Drove all night – no lights – going like blazes – lost 5 trucks over the bank – it was hell – over twice myself - each time complete capsize.
> *Thursday 24 April* – What a day – destroyed gun after tank action – pulled out
> *Friday 25 April* – pm arrived Athens – such a wonderful reception – 17 miles to olive grove – rest till 6 pm then 18 miles to beach – 11 pm dossed down in scrub – one blanket – cold frozen all night
> *Saturday 26 April* – In scrub all day – beach 9 pm – Kingston[133] – lost one boat.

In May 2003, my bus headed on westwards, under the steep faces of the hills rising from the sea – white limestone speckled with olive-green scrub. Soon we were crossing the deep-cut narrow canal at Corinth, taken by German paratroopers to cut off the Allied retreat in an ominous display of that method of assault, and then we were rolling into the Peloponnesus, past Mycenae and towards Nauplion.

In the final week of April 1941, the British and ANZAC commanders were intent on extricating their forces from the rapidly closing jaws of defeat. Their troops were streaming towards the evacuation points, harried from the air by a nearly unopposed enemy. The three principal places of embarkation for these weary, and in many cases wounded, men were the Peloponnesian ports of Nauplion, Kalamata, and Monemvasia, from which last point the bulk of the New Zealand forces would be taken off by the Royal Navy ship *Ajax* on 28 April.

Figure 40: Bourtzi island off Nauplion, seen from the author's hotel in May 2003 – the scene of the Sunderland operations in 1941.

The logbook had told me that, on 24 April 1941, T9046, with Frame, Paré, and Massam on the flight deck, had made the 90-minute crossing from Suda Bay on Crete to Nauplion, boarded 25 passengers, and flown back to Suda Bay in the earliest light of the following day. What these bare entries conceal is the confusion, chaos, and destruction at Nauplion during those two days.

From my balcony at the Dioscouri Hotel in Nauplion at dusk, I watched the orange gleam fade on the water around the island fortress of Bourtzi, just off the waterfront. The warm glow from the folds of the hills to the west darkened. The harbour was now flat calm and I understood the difficulties of alighting a flying boat at night in these conditions. It is quite impossible to judge the position of the surface – only a bland, featureless fuzziness presents itself to the viewer, and the approaching pilot. My father had great respect for these conditions, explaining to me in Tahiti days that a pilot needed to rely on shoreline features to judge height. Counterintuitively, the wise pilot ignored the water, turned sideways and judged height from the coconut trees on the shore. Needless to say, the Sunderland pilots had no coconut trees, or anything else to aid them, in the blinding dark of Pelopponesian bays in 1941.

```
93  400,000  12/39—McC & Co—51-5658
```

		OPERATIONS RECORD BOOK
of this form in K.R. and A.C.I., Pt. II., chapter XX., and Book.		Page 1
		of (Unit or Formation) No. 228 SQUADRON. R.A.F. No. of pages used for

Date	Time	Summary of Events
24/4	1910 2045	T 9046 Captain F/Lt Frame was ordered to fly to NAUPLIA BAY in the Bay of Argos to evacuate R.A.F. personnel believed to be in the district. On arrival just before dusk in was found the the R.A.F party had moved on. However, after considerable delay 25 passengers were taken on board including General Mac Cabe and one stretcher case: The Captain decided to wait until daybreak before making the takeoff:
24/4	0530 0730	At dawn F/Lt Frame T9046 found thatthe whole Bay was envelopped in dense black smoke caused byan ammunition ship and a troopship which had been bombed in the harbour the previous afternoon. After taxying round for a considerable time to maxpxrxaxa to find a clear petch the captain decided to make a blind take off on a course given to him by his navigator F/O Austin: The take off was accomplished without mishap and the evacuees whax landed at Suda Bay
24/4	1530 1930	L 9048 F/Lt Lamondwas ordered to escort two Imperial Flying Boats to Suda Bay. The Sunderland carried the luggage of the passengers of the Imperial Flying Boats,
25/4	1030 1140	L 9048 Captain P/Lt Lamond, 2nd pilot F/O Lylian,was ordered to search for a party of the R.A.F. believed to be in the Githeon area. A landing was made in the harbour of Githeon as people on the quayside waving were believed to be the party in question. After anchoring Greek officials arrived in rowing boats and explained in French that the R.A.F. had moved on to a bay a little further South West: One Greek Flight Leiutenant was taken aboard and the search resumed. On reaching the position indicated the aircraft was attracted by flashes from a hand mirror used by the ground party: After flying low over the position on two occasions it was confirmed that the people below were those the aircraft was seeking: A landingwas made and the aircraft anchored about 100 yds from the shore: Contact was made with the party which numbered 101 officers and men of 112 Squadron from Ixxixxx Janina. 52 of these were evacuated: The Captain of the aircraft left a message with the officer commanding that he would return to pick up the others if he received no other instructions If he did not return by 8 o'clock the remainder were to get away in the ciaque which was at their disposal: Aircraft landed the passengers at Suda Bay.

Figure 41: Excerpt from 228 Squadron ORB for 24–25 April 1941. This is the origin of the mistaken naming of 'General Mac Cabe' for the Australian general, Sir Iven Mackay, in subsequent accounts.

T9046 must have moored near Bourtzi to take on passengers brought out from the town. Tonight, it is illuminated for the tourists: lovers walk the promenade hand in hand, dogs and cats enticed out by the cool of the evening scamper about, a wedding at the church attracts a crowd of well-wishers and gawkers. On the waterfront is moored a palatial tourist-ship, all bulbous glass and white hull. I can just make out its name, *Seabourne Spirit*. An electric band plays under coloured lights on the open deck where bodies move to cover versions of 'Moon River', 'Jailhouse Rock', and the Platters' number, 'Only You'.

The predicament at Nauplion in the days and nights of 24–27 April 1941 is best gathered from the account of the naval officer sent by Admiral Cunningham to organise the evacuation. Admiral Baillie-Grohman, a passenger aboard T9046 a week earlier, took down first-hand accounts from survivors:

> . . . we beached in the forenoon of April 24th . . . at 1630, a Lt. Commander Clark arrived by truck from Athens to set up shop as principal beach-master. An hour later a Greek ammo ship (the *Nicolaos Georgios*) previously bombed blew up in Nauplion Bay and that helped to give the scene an authentic atmosphere . . .

At dusk on the 24th two Sunderlands – 230 Squadron's L2160 (Flight Lieutenant Woodward) and 228 Squadron's T9046 – landed in Nauplion Bay. That night, T9046 boarded 25 passengers, including the commander of the Australian rearguard, General Iven Mackay.[134] On 8 April, Mackay had been put in command of a force with orders to slow down the German advance in the Florina Valley, to the west of the New Zealanders fighting in the passes of Mount Olympus. Now, having led his Australian troops in a courageous though doomed action, the general was immaculately dressed but, to war correspondent Kenneth Slessor, 'looked worn and tired. His hair and neck were coated with dust. Dust in his eyes.'[135]

The record hints that T9046's high-ranking passengers were impatient to get away, and that it was a stubborn Flight Lieutenant Frame, indubitably in command of his Sunderland, who declined to take off until the earliest gleam of light the following morning. The general and his staff reluctantly spent the night moored in Nauplion Bay, amid burning ships. At 5.30 am, the first light revealed the full predicament of the Sunderland and its complement. The 228 Squadron ORB explains:

> At dawn Fl. Lt. Frame found that the whole Bay was enveloped in dense black smoke caused by an ammunition ship and a troopship which had been bombed in the harbour the previous afternoon. After taxiing around for a considerable time to find a clear patch the captain decided to make a blind take off on a course given to him by his navigator F/O Austin: the take off was accomplished without mishap and the evacuees were landed at Suda Bay.[136]

General Mackay had been a reluctant passenger on T9046, but

the change of plan proved fortuitous. Mackay's biographer records that there had been some uncertainty about the aircraft, so they decided to board the *Ulster Prince* at Nauplion. 'Then the plans were changed: there was a Sunderland flying-boat after all. Mackay and his ADC arrived at Suda Bay, Crete, at 6 am on ANZAC day, 1941.'[137] The initial preference would have been a very hazardous escape route for the Australian general, as German bombers caught the *Ulster Prince* at daylight on 25 April 'and by evening she had been reduced to a wreck, on fire for her whole length . . . the wreck now blocked the Harbour and denied access to ships larger than destroyers'.[138]

General Mackay's departure had been the result of a direct order from headquarters in Athens on 24 April that both he and General Freyberg were to leave by Sunderland that night. When Freyberg received the order, he was in a battle against German tanks at the Thermopylae pass. The general has described his response:

> I cabled back to G.H.Q. Athens, and told them I was being attacked by tanks . . . and asked who was to command the New Zealand troops if I left. I was given the answer of 'Movement Control'. I naturally went on with the battle. After that I never received an order as to my disposal.[139]

Later on 25 April, T9046 was back in the Peloponnesus – further west this time, at Kalamata, where a large group of RAF personnel were gathered for evacuation under Group Captain Lee.

Kalamata was in 1941 also home to Lawrence Durrell and his family. The writer told his American friend Henry Miller of that spring in the Peloponnesus:

> Now spring is coming this valley is getting beautiful and serene, encircled by snow caps, and raving with oranges. Last Sunday we walked up the dizziest mountain path to the snowline of our range and saw the great white snout of Taigetos in the valley beyond . . . [140]

But on 25 April, Durrell and his family, joining the exodus, scrambled aboard a caique for a perilous and uncomfortable crossing to Crete. Overhead, T9046 searched for the RAF evacuees and safe alighting areas. A measure of the chaos and of the German monopoly of the air was that T9046 was mistakenly fired on from the ground by those awaiting rescue, and the tail plane damaged. But contact was made with the RAF group and 'the Group Captain and 50 members of the party had come down from the hills. This party was boarded and flown back to Suda Bay.'[141]

That night, Henry Lamond, Alec's compatriot co-pilot, now in command of Sunderland T9048, which had earlier in the day carried a record number of passengers from Kalamata – 84 including crew – was sent back there to land in the dark. The aircraft crashed in the bay off Kalamata while attempting to alight. This incident, in which several crew members were killed, including the New Zealander John Lylian, is discussed more fully in Chapter 8.

In April 2005 I visited Kalamata, hoping to find even small traces or echoes of the events in 1941 – of the Sunderlands coming and going, of the battle two days later for the streets and waterfront in which the New Zealanders of 20 Battalion Reinforcements fought and died, and of the exploits of Sergeant Jack Hinton which earned him the Victoria Cross. I walked along the beach and made my way out to the end of the long breakwater where, on this still evening, I quietly saluted Lylian and the other casualties in T9048, the ruins of which lie out there in Homer's 'wine-dark sea'.

The following day I drove from Kalamata up the winding road through the jagged peaks and plunging ravines of the Taigetos mountains to Sparta on its plain, and on to the pretty port of Githeon, from which Henry Lamond's Sunderland had plucked grateful evacuees on 24 April. I understood why the Sunderlands flew respectfully around, not over, the mighty Taigetos, of which Kazantzakis' poet-friend, Sikelianos, wrote:

> From the peaks of Taygetos with ice forever
> gleaming silver . . . .[142]

Another New Zealand Sunderland skipper with 230 Squadron, and also an old Waitakian, Flight Lieutenant S.W.R. Hughes,[143] has left us a contemporary oral account of these days of evacuation from Greece. In a wartime radio interview Rochford Hughes, in an even-toned, matter-of-fact voice, told listeners in New Zealand of the work of the flying boats here, observing that it was 'an eerie business, flying about and landing in strange waters with not a light to help'.[144]

The dual responsibilities of the Sunderlands and their crews were noted in an official account of the campaign in Greece:

> While this evacuation was proceeding it was also necessary
> for our Sunderlands to carry out reconnaissance over the
> Mediterranean throughout the hours of daylight, to guard
> against possible raids by the Italian Navy against our
> transports and ships engaged in the evacuation. Thus in
> addition to spending the hours of daylight in reconnaissance,
> the Sunderlands went on to take part in the rescue work
> at night. Their Captains and crews therefore went without
> sleep or rest, while engaged in the most delicate, exhausting
> work.[145]

The final word on the role of the flying boats in the evacuation of
Greece might be left to the RAF's commanding officer there:

> A reference to the evacuation would not be complete without
> a tribute being paid to the flying boats, both of the RAF and
> BOAC. These boats carried out magnificent work ferrying
> parties of airmen and soldiers . . . A number of their flights
> were carried out in conditions of the utmost danger, and,
> throughout, the pilots and crews displayed the utmost
> gallantry and devotion to duty.[146]

It seems that the 'getting out' of Greece was better handled than
the 'getting in'. General Freyberg's son, Paul Freyberg, who served
in the Middle East theatre, gives the raw statistics: out of 62,000
British and Commonwealth troops in Greece, some 46,000 were
evacuated, 1000 killed, 1000 wounded, and 14,000 taken prisoner.
As to the 'getting in', Paul Freyberg wrote bluntly that 'There can
be little doubt that the decision to break off pursuit of the beaten
Italian Army in Tripolitania in favour of the Greek expedition was
one of the biggest British military blunders of the Second World
War.'[147]

As a military judgement, that seems right. However, as will be
suggested in the next chapter, this conclusion must be set against
another dimension of the war in 1941. The need to 'sacrifice'
fighting forces to preserve and advance other interests judged to be
of sufficient importance in the overall conduct of a war is one of
the heaviest burdens borne by wartime leaders. As the language of
military tombstones reminds us, defensive wars *inherently* represent
a decision that the 'sacrifice' of warriors is justified by the 'political'
claims of 'liberty' or 'freedom from oppression'. Of course, soldiers
and citizens have a right to expect that there will not be *needless*

loss of life and treasure, but it will not be a sufficient objection to a military operation to show that it had no, or very little, chance of purely military success.

The defence of 'higher interests' aside – and more will be said soon about the transatlantic dimension of the Greek adventure – the British Prime Minister may himself have subsequently come to judge the 'Lustre' decision unfavourably. Colville reported Churchill's comment to him made 'while dressing for dinner' on 28 September 1941:

> So far the Government had made only one error of judgment: Greece. He [Churchill] had instinctively had doubts. We could and should have defended Crete and advised the Greek Government to make the best terms it could.[148]

General Freyberg summed up the pull-out from Greece in an Order of the Day from Crete, where he rested with his troops on 1 May 1941:

> The withdrawal from Greece has now been completed. It has been a difficult operation. A smaller force held a much larger force at bay for over a month and then withdrew from an open beach. This rearguard battle and the withdrawal has been a great feat of arms. The fighting qualities and steadiness of the troops were beyond praise . . . [149]

7. The Americans Are Coming?

My interest in the activity of American observers in the Mediterranean theatre in 1941 was awakened by some entries in Alec's logbook for the first week in May 1941. He flew T9046 from Alexandria to Lake Timsah, then on to the Sea of Galilee – the fresh-water lake of biblical fame around whose shores Jesus recruited disciples and performed several miracles – and then to Basra in Iraq. The purpose of the journey is made clear by the entry on 8 May: a seven-hour evacuation flight from Basra to Lake Timsah for which the passengers are noted as '15 hospital cases – Colonel Rooseveld [sic]'.

As T9046 flew to Basra, Churchill was addressing a sulky House of Commons on the reverses in Greece and Rommel's rampage eastwards towards the Nile. All his debating skills were required to explain the underestimate of Rommel's threat:

> That was a mistake. But anyone who supposes that there will not be mistakes in war is very foolish. I draw a distinction between mistakes. There is a mistake which comes through daring, which I call a mistake towards the enemy in which you must always sustain your commanders, by sea, land or air. There are mistakes from the safety-first principle, mistakes of turning away from the enemy; and they require a far more acid consideration.[150]

The Prime Minister painted a grim picture of the difficulties ahead, but ended on a note of optimism:

> When I look back on the perils which have been overcome, upon the great mountain waves in which the gallant ship has driven, when I remember all that has gone wrong, and remember also all that has gone right, I feel sure we have no need to fear the tempest. Let it roar, and let it rage. We shall come through.

Harold Nicolson was present and described the performance in his diary:

He holds the House from the first moment. He stands there in his black conventional suit with the huge watch-chain. He is very amusing. He is very frank ... As Winston goes out of the Chamber towards the Members' Lobby, there is a spontaneous burst of cheering which is taken up outside. He looks pleased.[151]

Figure 42: President Roosevelt's son, Jimmy Roosevelt (centre), steps from an RAF Lockheed Lodestar aircraft in the Middle East, 1941.

My suspicion that Alec's passenger in T9046 might have been James ('Jimmy') Roosevelt,[152] the son of United States President Franklin Delano Roosevelt (FDR), was confirmed when I made inquiries at the Franklin D. Roosevelt Library at Hyde Park, New York, and was sent a copy of a telegram from the American Ambassador in Cairo to the Secretary of State dated 8 May 1941:

> Following for the President and Mrs James Roosevelt: 'Arrived safely Cairo. All well here. Press reports father unwell. Would appreciate any and all family news. All love. Jimmy'

No doubt, then, that 'Colonel Rooseveld' was the lanky Jimmy Roosevelt. Further details of his travels at that time can be found in his own account, published in 1959:

In April, 1941, less than a week after my second marriage – I
was on my way around the world on a military-diplomatic
mission for Father. In company with Major Gerald C.
Thomas . . . I visited the Philippines, China, Burma, India,
Iraq, Egypt, Crete, Palestine, and various beleaguered African
outposts.[153]

The President's son explained that the ostensible purpose of the
mission was to observe military requirements and the performance
of American-supplied weapons. But Jimmy had a further task:

. . . a rather delicate one, which had been entrusted to me by
my Father. I was to call on heads of state or governing officials
in the places we visited . . . I was to assure them verbally in
Father's name that, although the United States was not in the
war against Hitler and Mussolini, we were doing all that a
neutral nation properly could for the allies . . . in effect I was
telling them, 'Hang on, help may be coming'.

Joseph Persico, in his helpful account of Roosevelt's 'secret war',
makes Jimmy's briefing from the President more direct, and the
message to be delivered stronger:

Behind closed doors in his private study he told his son, 'This
must be completely confidential. The Congress, the press and
the public would never approve my message, but I consider it
critical to the morale of the countries we must support' . . .
In effect Jimmy was to tell these leaders, 'Hang on until we
get in'.[154]

Jimmy's role was officially denied by the President. A press conference
on 2 May 1941 included this exchange containing the masterfully
bland lie required by national security:

Q. Mr President, anything new on the appointment of a
minister to New Zealand?
THE PRESIDENT: Minister to where?
Q. New Zealand
THE PRESIDENT: No, I haven't heard a word
Q. Mr President, can you tell us anything about the mission
of your son, Captain James Roosevelt?
THE PRESIDENT: About what?
Q. About the mission that he is performing?

THE PRESIDENT: I haven't the faintest idea. You would have to ask the Marine Corps.[155]

In reality, Captain Roosevelt, who can be seen stepping off an RAF aircraft in the photograph, had a ringside seat for the Middle East fighting, and the Alexandria-based Sunderlands of 230 and 228 Squadrons had the task of getting him in and out of the battle zones. He had been on Crete just before the German invasion and was airlifted out on 230 Squadron's heavily laden Sunderland T9050 under Wing Commander Francis:

> . . . on one such trip Wg Cdr Francis in T9050 airlifted a total of 74 men apart from his ten crew back to Egypt, including Captain James Roosevelt, son of the USA's President who being ostensibly 'neutral' had been a 'military observer and adviser' in Greece.[156]

Jimmy's own description of his arrival in Crete gives the flavour of his activities:

> We flew into Crete – over strong objections from the British, who were worried about our security – after the Nazis had begun their aerial assault on that island. Coming into Suda Bay, where we were to land, our relatively slow Sunderland flying boat actually took a few shots at a Nazi patrol vessel, and then had to dodge Luftwaffe fighters as we made our landing on the water. I was deeply impressed by the heroic King George of Greece, who, in uniform, was with the defending troops on Crete, and by the coolness of the British, who were taking the ordeal as if it were some adventuresome picnic. The British, however, hustled us out of Crete the day after we arrived – and none too soon, for, right after our departure, the aerial envelopment of the island by parachutists and glider-borne troops began.[157]

In Iraq in May, Jimmy and Major Thomas, in addition to spreading FDR's reassurances as instructed, and enduring strafing by German fighters,[158] may well have been examining the suitability of Basra as the point of entry for the tanks and fighters soon to arrive from America to reinforce British forces in North Africa. This plan for replenishment of Wavell's depleted resources had been foreshadowed in Churchill's instruction of 10 April to the Secretary of State for India that 'I shall be greatly interested in the plan you will make in the next few days for making Basra a great American Assembly point'.[159] The proposal was put to President Roosevelt in Averell Harriman's telegram for FDR from London on 14 April 1941, which message throws light also on the intimacy of US–British relations in the period:

> For the purpose of evolving plans for the aggressive defence of Libya and Egypt Churchill had an all day meeting yesterday with Chief of Air Force, First Sea Lord, General Dill and Foreign Minister and it was decided to inaugurate active air and naval campaign to sever Hitler's line of supply to Tripoli ... The development of Basra or Suez as base for imports and assembly of as many of our aircraft as is possible with as many mechanics and engineers from the United States is urgently requested by Air Force Chief.[160]

The follow-up was FDR's administrative order declaring the Persian Gulf and Basra to be outside the war zone, and therefore not covered by the ban imposed by the Neutrality Acts on the transport of war *matériel* in American ships.

Now, on 9 May 1941, seven months before the attack on Pearl Harbor, Jimmy Roosevelt, in Cairo courtesy of 228 Squadron's Sunderland, talked to the American press and was quoted as saying that the United States, 'except for sending troops, already is in the war'. The *New York Times* reported his advocacy of 'an American shipping pool to provide bottoms . . . to bring vital military supplies to Egypt', adding that 'He will meet General Sir Archibald P. Wavell tomorrow and plans to stay several weeks in the area to investigate the military situation . . . '[161] The isolationist movement in America still had momentum and seized on the ambivalence of Jimmy Roosevelt's reported statements. In the same issue the *New York Times* carried criticism of his 'already in the war' remark from Representative Hamilton Fish Jr, who denied that the President's son, 'as a soldier', had the right to make such a comment, adding that 'he was not a military expert'.

The intimacy of the 'American connection', and the manner in which the American 'observers' acted as go-betweens for FDR and Churchill, is illustrated by a personal letter to Churchill, handwritten by Jimmy Roosevelt on his way home from his travels, on board the BOAC Empire flying boat *Clare* on 16 June 1941.[162] The letterhead is 'Government House, Gambia, West Africa', where Jimmy, travelling with 'Dickie' Mountbatten on the latter's way home after the loss of the destroyer *Kelly* off Crete, had been forced down when their Sunderland lost an engine.[163]

My Dear Prime Minister,

Until the last minute I had hoped to have the pleasure and privilege of seeing you again in London. But at Father's request I am turning off at Lisbon for New York and according to Averell Harriman coming over later I hope. I am asking Dickie Mountbatten, who has been a delightful companion these last two weeks, to give you this note. We have had an opportunity to go over several ideas resulting from observations in West Africa and Middle East concerning the situation here. Perhaps you would let him give the general outline as I shall to Father . . .

Some day soon I hope too, that we can review the battle of Crete. It was a greatly appreciated privilege to view and review it so close at hand. It certainly was not lost if the spirit of valor displayed by the fighting forces inspires, as I feel it will, the whole Middle East Command. And above all it proved that the enemy can never make a sea-borne attack on England as long as the Royal Navy does the sort of completely successful job it did around Crete. The losses were of course heavy but soon we may hope no British forces will have to fight with practically no fighting air support or protection. It was a grand job and history I believe will record it.

To you always all of us send our real affection and great respect. We may 'off the record' hope to be allowed to serve and aid under your leadership more and more in the days to come.

Yours most sincerely
James Roosevelt

It is difficult to overestimate the importance for Churchill of America's attitude to the war in the period between the fall of France in June 1940 and the full entry of the US into the war, precipitated by the Japanese attack on Pearl Harbor in December 1941. Even the Prime Minister's famous 'We will fight them on the beaches' rallying speech on 4 June 1940, after Dunkirk, recognised that the resistance he called for so passionately and eloquently could only hold the enemy 'until, in God's good time, the New World, with all its power and might, steps forth to the rescue and liberation of the old'.[164]

Given the supportive attitude of Roosevelt and several of his key advisers to the British cause, why was practical and effective American support for the fight against Hitler so difficult to enlist and to deliver? The answer may be found in the role of 'public opinion' in the American political process as understood by FDR. Joe Lash's illuminating 1976 study of the relations between Roosevelt and Churchill between 1939 and 1941 is the indispensable guide to the subtleties and nuances of the process which saw a supposedly neutral America become first a covert supplier, then the proclaimed 'arsenal of democracy', and finally the active protector of the lines of supply, before full belligerency was triggered by the Japanese attack on Pearl Harbor.

Both the personal styles of Roosevelt and Churchill and the structures of the respective political systems within which they worked made 'public opinion' a more immediate and sensitive issue for the President than for the Prime Minister. Churchill relished the independence of the leader in war and mocked the 'ear to the ground' posture in relation to public opinion. Roosevelt's philosophy encompassed a more cautious and interactive approach, as seen in his speech to the Commonwealth Club in 1932:

> Government includes the art of formulating a policy and using the political technique to attain so much of that policy as will receive general support, persuading, leading, sacrificing, teaching always, because the greatest duty of a statesman is to educate.[165]

As to political structures, the British Ambassador in Washington in 1940, Lord Lothian, reported that 'public opinion' assumed a greater and more immediate role in American affairs because of the balance of constitutional powers between the executive and legislative branches of government. When, as so often occurred, the balance of powers produced stalemate, public opinion became the tie-breaker. In the British system, however, 'the Government of the day, provided it can keep the support of its own majority and does not provoke by its policy a violent agitation in the country, can make its own policy prevail'.[166]

A Roper poll taken in September 1939 showed that 37.5 per cent of Americans thought that the United States should 'take no sides and stay out of the war entirely, but offer to sell armaments to anyone on a "cash-and-carry" basis'. Nearly 30 per cent agreed that their country should 'have nothing to do with any warring country – don't even trade with them on a cash-and-carry basis'.[167] These were worrying figures, and the White House observer on the spot, Robert Sherwood, commented:

> The all-out isolationist faction which would have 'nothing to do with any warring country' was close to thirty per cent and this remained a pretty constant figure through all of the opinion tests that were made over such issues as Selective Service, the destroyers-for-bases deal, Lend Lease, etc.[168]

Even after Roosevelt's renomination and election for an unprecedented third term in November 1940, the passage through Congress of the Lend-Lease Bill in March 1941, and the rise of the President's popularity to 72 per cent in the polls, it could not be assumed that the administration's assistance to the British cause was irreversible. Lash cites an influential British Foreign Office analyst at that time as noting America's dislike of foreign entanglements and, less charitably, the unwillingness of its people to acknowledge the responsibilities of material privilege. The analyst warned that 'it would be unwise to assume that, in certain circumstances, the Americans would be incapable of checking their present helpful trend. The Americans are coming on well, but they are not yet in the bag . . . '[169]

'Isolationists' and 'defeatists' were still about in American places, both popular and official. The most notable of the former was the stellar Colonel Charles A. Lindbergh, the aviator who had captured imaginations with his transatlantic flight in 1927. On 23 April 1941, Lindbergh addressed a large crowd at an 'America First' rally in New York, telling the throng that 'we cannot win this war for England, regardless of how much assistance we send'.[170] Officialdom provided the example of Colonel Truman Smith of the US Army, who angered the Secretary of War, Henry Stimson, by expressing the view that the British expedition to Greece was based on political meddling rather than sound military judgement. Stimson relates in his diary how he reprimanded Smith, adding that he had discussed the matter with Colonel Donovan, who 'reminded me that the decision to send British troops to Greece had not been made by Cabinet or Churchill at all but by Wavell himself and that Donovan had been present when it was made'.[171]

The provision of American war *matériel* for the British war effort involved a further dilemma in addition to its possible conflict with neutrality. Every warplane and every tank sent across the Atlantic represented a loss to the American capacity to fight alone if British resistance collapsed. The same grim calculus had faced Churchill before the fall of France, when the great French need was for more British fighter aircraft. In spite of his Francophile view, Churchill adamantly refused to provide the fighter squadrons on the basis that they were indispensable to repulsing the German attack on the British homeland which would surely follow a collapse in France. Clearly, the Prime Minister was not confident that France would be successfully defended. Similarly, an essential pre-condition for the continuation and extension of the US supply to Britain was an American perception that the British military effort was wholehearted, and capable of withstanding the German attack.

When, after his 'arsenal of democracy' speech on 17 December 1940, FDR sent his trusted adviser Harry Hopkins to London to get relations between the leaders on a practical and more personal basis, it was with the message that the President was 'very stubborn about the British and the war effort. We want to help them to the limit, but the President is going to insist that they must prove that they are doing their best before we go all out for them . . . '[172]

Hopkins arrived in London on 9 January 1941, having flown by Pan American Boeing 314 Clipper flying boat to Lisbon, and thence by Empire flying boat to Poole on the south coast of England. His report to Roosevelt on the first meeting with Churchill left no doubt as to the Prime Minister's assessment of the military prospects in Greece: 'He thinks Greece is lost . . . he believes Hitler will permit Mussolini to go only so far downhill – and is now preparing for the attack which must bring inevitable results.'[173] The significance of Greece in the minds of Roosevelt and Hopkins is underlined by the importance it is accorded in the latter's reporting from London to the White House:

> The PM impatient – prodding Wavell – but ever giving him
> his confident support – but Greece must be supported for
> political reasons and Wavell grudgingly agrees, for these are
> explicit orders from the Minister of Defence.[174]

'Lord Root of the Matter', as Churchill significantly dubbed Hopkins, was intensively wooed by the British leader during his visit, both socially and politically. There were dinners, racy company, and much talk accompanied by liquor. Hopkins and Churchill found they had good 'chemistry', and at a public meeting in Glasgow the American emissary quoted reassuringly from the Book of Ruth: 'Whither thou goest, I will go . . . even to the end.'

Hopkins returned to Washington an enthusiastic supporter of Churchill personally, and of the British cause generally. His position as the President's personal friend and 'live-in' adviser meant that he could short-circuit the State Department and service bureaucracies when Roosevelt entrusted the *de facto* administration and prioritisation of the Lend-Lease programme to him. As Sherwood explains:

> The extraordinary fact was that the second most important individual in the United States Government during the most critical period of the world's greatest war had no legitimate official position nor even any desk of his own except a card table in his bedroom. However, the bedroom was in the White House.[175]

Yet Churchill still had work to do to translate American sentiment into delivered hardware. Britain needed to hold the American administration to its progressive assurances about material help, and to prevent slippage as political difficulties were encountered. In this regard it was important for Britain to be seen to honour commitments made, even where circumstances might have become problematic. This had particular relevance for the situation in Greece, to whose government the British had pledged assistance in the event of attack. The two critical Cabinet decisions in London were that of 10 January 1941, emphasising the 'political importance' of aid to Greece, and that of 11 February, which determined that 'it was of the first political importance to provide Greece with the fullest possible support'.[176]

Churchill's own view of the connection between the ill-fated expedition to Greece and the American readiness to 'bend', and then overturn, the rules restricting their assistance to the British effort is suggested in this paragraph of his subsequent account:

> There is no doubt that the Mussolini-Hitler crime of overrunning Greece, and our effort to stand against tyranny and save what we could from its claws, appealed profoundly to the people of the United States, and above all to the great man who led them.[177]

Armed with knowledge from Enigma decryption that Greece was the first objective of the German Balkans campaign, the 11 February Cabinet meeting explicitly instructed Wavell to give assistance to Greece 'priority over continuing the advance as far as Tripoli'.[178] The Cabinet also instructed Anthony Eden and General Dill to visit Cairo, for discussions with Wavell and Longmore, and then Athens, where they were to offer 'immediate reinforcements' to the government in Greece.

The pair began their journey two days later by special train to Plymouth, where a Sunderland waited at Mount Batten. Eden mused: 'Hardly a secret departure, the train being drawn up at No1 platform, a space railed off and a crowd assembled'.[179] Their flight, in Flight Lieutenant Havyatt's Sunderland of Australia's 10 Squadron, was an adventure of its own. The weather was turbulent and the passengers made ill, and so low was fuel that not only did they cut across Portuguese air space, but nearly had to alight helplessly in the straits off Gibraltar. Eden contemplated internment or drowning: 'We should not have made it if our pilot had not been really splendid and the navigator and every member of the crew.'[180]

It is interesting to see Churchill's own retrospective list of the five great 'climacterics' of the war: the fall of France, the Battle of Britain, Lend-Lease, the German attack on Russia, and the Japanese attack on Pearl Harbor. The military setbacks in Greece and Crete (and later successes in North Africa) did not, in the Prime Minister's mind, warrant a place on the list except as subsumed under the Lend-Lease heading. For Churchill, in both prospect and retrospect, securing American assistance was the primary objective in that phase of the war.

The struggle for the Lend-Lease programme, under which Britain could order modern American war supplies free of the 'cash and carry' requirement, needed all FDR's persuasiveness. At a press conference on 17 December 1940, Roosevelt had used a homely metaphor to describe his approach to military aid to Britain: 'Well, let me give you an illustration: Suppose my neighbour's home catches fire, and I have got a length of garden hose four or five hundred feet away . . . ' The President developed this idea, but stressed that 'the people of Europe who are defending themselves do not ask us to do their fighting'. He declared that 'We must be the great arsenal of democracy.'[181] Across the Atlantic, in February 1941, Churchill carefully echoed the implicit reassurance that Americans would not be sent to fight in Europe with his 'Give us the tools and we will finish the job' speech.

Robert Sherwood's valuable study of the wartime papers of Harry Hopkins observes of Roosevelt's 'garden hose' approach:

> I believe it may accurately be said that with that neighbourly analogy Roosevelt won the fight for Lend Lease. There were to be two months of some of the bitterest debate in American history, but through it all the American people as a whole maintained the conviction that there couldn't be anything very radical or dangerous in the President's proposal to lend our garden hose to the British, who were fighting so heroically against such fearful odds.[182]

At Churchill's end, however, the success of the homely analogy depended on there actually being 'heroic fighting against fearful odds' – in short, a *convincing* fire – and it is not surprising to find that this need entered the calculations of the British War Cabinet in the decision to send a force to Greece.

On 8 March 1941, the Lend-Lease Bill was passed by Congress. Under the measure, the US Government would itself order war *matériel* required by the British, and lease it to Britain. No cash would be required. American war supplies of all kinds were thus for the first time reliably available in quantity. But a major problem remained: how to get the *matériel* safely across the Atlantic through the U-boat packs? There were two aspects to the problem: first, British convoy protection was too stretched across the Atlantic expanse to be effective; and second, British shipping was depleted and the US Neutrality Acts prevented the carriage of war *matériel* by American ships into 'combat zones'. These were the two outstanding supply problems for Churchill in March 1941.

Harry Hopkins and Jimmy Roosevelt were not the only emissaries sent by the American President to reassure the British leaders of US moral and material support while pressing for demonstrations of military initiative. Now we should consider the activity of a third agent of the President, William Donovan, who quickly came to be seen in London as a possible answer to the British supply problems. With a law degree from Columbia, where he had been a star quarter-back on the football team, Donovan had earned a Medal of Honor, and the nick-name 'Wild Bill', in World War I. In 1941 Donovan became Roosevelt's 'Co-ordinator of Intelligence' (COI), and subsequently the first head of the Office of Special Operations (OSS) and, after the war, the architect of its successor, the Central Intelligence Agency (CIA).[183] In 1940 the President had asked Donovan to visit Britain to report on the capacity and resolve of the British to resist the German war machine. In early 1941, Donovan – whom FDR liked to call 'My Secret Legs' – was again in London.

My compatriot Tony Simpson comes the closest to pin-pointing the role of Donovan in providing essential reassurance for FDR that, to Prime Minister Churchill's undoubted political will to withstand German might, was added the requisite military capacity and strategic determination. Simpson observes in his 1981 study of the battle for Crete: 'The message Donovan conveyed to Churchill . . . was clear. If supplies were to continue to flow across the Atlantic, then the notion that Britain was a spent force must be erased from the consciousness of the American public.'[184]

The reason for Donovan's first visit to London, in July 1940, appears to have been the desire of his close friend, the newly appointed Secretary for the Navy, Frank Knox, to procure for the US Government first-hand and reliable information on the war as it looked from London. No doubt there was presidential approval of the mission and of the choice of FDR's Columbia Law School classmate and military hero as emissary, but the President was not at this stage the prime mover. 'Wild Bill' left New York by Pan American Clipper flying boat – the new Boeing 314 – on 14 July for London via Lisbon.

Hurriedly organised, and intensely annoying to US Ambassador Joe Kennedy in London, the visit brought Donovan into contact with the British Security Intelligence Service (SIS) and its head, Colonel (later Sir) Stewart Menzies (eccentrically pronounced 'Mingis'), usually simply called 'C', who briefed his American visitor very fully on all aspects of the war from a security point of view. A round of visits to leading political and military leaders in London followed, including King George VI and, of course, Winston Churchill.

Following this comprehensive introduction to British ways, Donovan left England on 3 August 1940 in BOAC's Empire flying boat *Clare*, pressed into transatlantic service in green and blue camouflage patches. The British Overseas Airways Corporation (BOAC), newly formed in succession to Imperial Airways, treated its first translatlantic passengers in style: they were farewelled by the Secretary of State for Air, Sir Archibald Sinclair, who supplied champagne for the journey.

Donovan's message on his return to Washington in early August was that the British had high morale but were short of equipment. He met the President on 9 August, and lent his weight to the consummation of the 'destroyers-for-bases' deal under which the US would transfer to Britain 50 old destroyers for convoy protection work in return for the granting of leases to British bases in the British West Indies. He also procured from his law firm imaginative advice to get around some constitutional difficulties blocking the deal,[185] which was duly announced to the House of Commons in London on 5 September.

Donovan's second trip to London, in December 1940, arose out of the confidence created on both sides of the Atlantic by the tone and outcome of the first. This time, the President himself, fortified by his election victory on 5 November 1940 over the Republican presidential candidate, Wendell Willkie, and reassured by Donovan's favourable reception in London and by the American public, was actively involved. This second mission called for on-the-spot observation of the military situation in the Middle East and Balkans, which were emerging as the principal active theatres in the conflict. One commentator reports Donovan's own confirmation that, although nominally the representative of Navy Secretary Knox, he was 'in reality the agent of the President' and that he was 'to collect information on conditions and prospects and, more importantly, to impress on everyone the resolution of the American Government and people to see the British through'.[186]

On 6 December 1940, Donovan and C's man in Washington, William Stephenson, set out for London via Bermuda, where bad weather held up progress for eight days, and Lisbon. They arrived in England on 16 December and two days later Donovan had a long lunch with Churchill at Downing Street, at which it was settled that the American emissary would be taken fully into British confidence and given every opportunity to observe operations at first hand and interview commanders at the highest level in the field. The Prime Minister deputed Colonel Vivian Dykes of the War Cabinet Secretariat to accompany Donovan to the Mediterranean. Anthony Cave Brown's colourfully written account reports the sequel:

> On New Year's Eve 1940, a four-engine Sunderland maritime reconnaissance flying boat carrying Donovan took off in a cloud of spume from Plymouth Sound, climbed over the

Lizard, and set course over the Western Approaches out to the ten-degree line to avoid the Focke-Wulf Kondors. At that point the captain turned south towards the first of the Empire's great coaling ports and military bastions, Gibraltar.[187]

The red carpet treatment for 'Wild Bill' began immediately:

> To make German interception more difficult, the flight lasted from dusk until dawn at Gibraltar, and to make it more agreeable, Lord Louis Mountbatten had sent a hamper containing Donovan's birthday dinner – he became fifty eight while flying through cirrus clouds over the western fringes of the Bay of Biscay. The hamper contained three bottles of a Moselle, a flask of hot turtle soup, fresh lobster, cold pheasant, and Stilton cheese and Bath Olivers. It was served beautifully by the orderly in a white mess jacket with gleaming brass buttons and white gloves.

For the next two months Donovan and Dykes criss-crossed the Mediterranean war theatre, taking in the besieged Malta, Cairo, the Western Desert in Libya, Greece, Belgrade, and Baghdad. Donovan was 'usually curled up in the tail of the aircraft, wrapped in travelling rugs and the long sheepskin trench coat he bought at Cordings in Piccadilly before leaving London'.[188]

Donovan's minder, 'Dumbie' Dykes, was an able and popular official who, in late 1941 and throughout 1942, became a key player in British/American planning in Washington. His talent for mimicry – sometimes at the expense of the great – amused his colleagues, as it must have entertained 'Wild Bill' on his Mediterranean travels.[189] The diary of his travels with Donovan in the Mediterranean and Balkans early in 1941 is a valuable source. On 15 January they had a bumpy ride in a Sunderland from Alexandria to Athens with Air Marshal Longmore. They visited the Acropolis before seeing leading Greek military and political figures. Dykes told his diary:

> He [Donovan] told me he had impressed on them that the US would see the Allies through; the debates in Congress on the Lease and Loan Bill are only concerned with the form in which executive authority is to be exercised and not on the principle of giving aid to Britain.[190]

The following day Dykes reported that the leading Greek general,

Alexander Papagos, had 'rather changed his attitude during the night (as a result of his talk with Donovan?)[191] and was now more disposed to favour acceptance of our offer of troops'.

The US Ambassador in Athens, Lincoln MacVeagh, although miffed that Donovan was to stay with British hosts, found his compatriot impressive: 'A fine type of American ... Yet since he is getting a bit stout, one might think him a mere "bon papa", if it were not for those bright blue eyes.'[192] Donovan's advocacy of British intervention in Greece continued with MacVeagh, who recorded that 'he thinks that a war here is inevitable, with Germany as well as Italy, and advisable too'. The interventionist view was reported in a message to Washington, with the ambassador recording that he drew on Donovan's views, 'but not naming him directly. He OK'd it before I sent it'. Writing privately to President Roosevelt on 19 January, MacVeagh sang Donovan's praises: 'He has been particularly useful not only as a prominent American fresh from home, but as a Republican, in impressing these people with the unanimity as well as the importance of our attitude towards the war.'[193]

Back in Cairo in February, Donovan again had the ear of Wavell and Longmore and was pressing the case for intervention in Greece. Dykes reported on a meeting on 8 February:

> He put over very well his idea of looking at the Mediterranean not as an east-west corridor, but as a no-man's land between two opposing fronts. The north-south conception seemed to strike Wavell very forcibly, and he was clearly impressed by Donovan's insistence on the need for keeping a foothold in the Balkans.[194]

On 19 February, just hours before the arrival of Foreign Secretary Anthony Eden from the War Cabinet in London, Dykes reported:

> Wavell showed me a paper from which it was clear that he had made up his mind to leap in as soon as possible in Salonika ... He showed the same paper to Donovan, who dined with him alone that night. I think his judgment had been considerably influenced by Donovan's advocacy, as it was a very finely balanced question to decide. [195]

Eden and General Dill had flown from Malta to Suda Bay and on to the Nile at Gezira in Cairo aboard 230 Squadron's Sunderland

N9029 (Flying Officer Alan Lywood), with the observant Dundas Bednall as second officer:

> Just off Crete an aircraft was reported shadowing us but fortunately no attack followed. Anthony Eden's hat, a black Homburg, was his 'trademark' and we all took turns to wear the celebrated headgear when the Minister was viewing the world from the cockpit! He wrote a most kind letter of thanks to the crew, with a bottle of whisky for Alan.[196]

After their weather-delayed journey from London, Eden and Dill arrived in Cairo on 19 February to Wavell's jesting greeting, 'You have been a long time coming'. They met Donovan that night and Eden recorded that the American

> was able to give me a first-hand account of recent developments. His blunt speech in those countries had been useful and I was grateful to him for waiting several days to see me. I asked him to send the President a message emphasising that any action we might take in the Mediterranean would overstrain our shipping resources and inviting him to help if he could.[197]

Donovan's advocacy was further exercised before these new arrivals. At British Middle East headquarters in Cairo, he had lengthy discussions with Wavell and was asked to attend the critical discussions on plans to send an expedition to Greece. These took place between 20 and 22 February 1941 and involved Wavell, his air and naval chiefs Longmore and Cunningham, and Eden and Dill. This summary of Donovan's role in the discussions is drawn from telegraphed reports from the American legation in Cairo:

> Donovan favoured British help to Greece. He was present with the British leaders when the decision was taken to send not only supplies but also British soldiers back on to the continent to help their Greek ally. Not unappreciative of the value of his support, they asked him to go to London to present his study of the Mediterranean before the Council of War.[198]

The gist of his argument that Greece should be the priority was summarised by Dykes: 'Britain has kept her in the fight and discouraged her from coming to terms ... Britain has a *moral* obligation to Greece. This policy would be sound *psychologically* for its effect on Germany, and on opinion in U.S.A.'[199]

The ensuing report to London from Wavell, Longmore and Cunningham, and Eden and Dill – all represented as agreeing – may well have been the crucial and determinative step in the decision to send an expedition to Greece. Eden's telegram to Churchill urged that the risks of the expedition should be accepted: 'that is the conviction we all hold here'. Dill reported similarly, mentioning specifically Donovan's view: 'He clearly thinks that help for Greece is urgent.'[200]

With their work done, Donovan and Dykes took the train from Cairo to Alexandria on Saturday, 22 February, lodging at the Cecil Hotel. There, the travelling pair met the Australian Prime Minister, Robert Menzies, who apparently attempted to assert priority for places on a Sunderland. Dykes reports 'Wild Bill's' response verbatim, and one almost hears the famed mimicry: 'Get this straight – we can't be euchred out of our seats by any goddam Prime Minister – we have got work to do and we are in a hurry.'[201] The following morning they boarded 228 Squadron's Sunderland L5807, with the squadron's commander, Nicholetts, at the controls and Lylian and Goldfinch on the flight deck, and took off at 8.45 for Malta. The journey on to Gibraltar the following day was a battle against head winds. Dykes told his diary: 'it seemed as if we would never reach Gibraltar. The pilot was obviously getting rather worried – counting lifebelts! – and by the time we finally came down at Gibraltar at 3.30 we had only fifteen minutes' petrol left.'[202]

On 2 March, still aboard L5807, the pair flew from Gibraltar to Mount Batten. Other passengers on this flight were Admiral A.L.StG. Lyster, commander of the aircraft-carrier squadron in the Mediterranean and planner of the successful attack on the Italian fleet in Taranto Harbour, along with Colonel Beattie and Commander Buzzard.[203] A month later this Sunderland, which Alec had delivered to Pembroke Dock from Rochester just before the outbreak of war, would burn to destruction in Kalafrana Bay, Malta.

On 10 March, with 'Wild Bill' back in London, Churchill sent a 'personal and most secret' message for President Roosevelt in these terms:

> I must now tell you what we have resolved about Greece. Although it was no doubt tempting to try to push on from Benghazi to Tripoli ... we have felt it our duty to stand with the Greeks who have declared to us their resolve, even

alone, to resist the German invader. Our Generals Wavell and Dill, who have accompanied Mr Eden to Cairo, after heart-searching discussions with us, believe we have a good fighting chance. We are therefore sending the greater part of the Army of the Nile to Greece, and are reinforcing to the utmost possible in the air ... Mr President, you can judge these hazards for yourself ... I must thank you for the magnificent work done by Donovan in his prolonged tour of Balkans and Middle East. He has carried with him throughout an animating, heart-warming flame ... [204]

In Cairo, Eden had urged Churchill and the War Cabinet that attention be given to publicity on Donovan's return to England. He signalled the Prime Minister:

He will I know make every effort on our behalf with the United States Government by explaining from first hand knowledge our difficulties over shipping, naval escorts and supply of equipment and aircraft required in this theatre ... From our standpoint it is important that through information given to American correspondents in London, the American Press should be able to inform their public opinion ... [205]

Donovan's influence at the Cairo end of the decision-making process is emphasised in Eden's message:

I found Colonel Donovan waiting for me in Cairo on his return from his tour of the Balkans and Middle East. You know (? Data) [sic] he held and his recommendation to the President. I am impressed by the help he has given us. May I suggest that on his return to London ... we show him every attention and express our gratitude in any way possible.[206]

A copy of Donovan's report on his recent tour of the Middle East was provided to Churchill on 6 March, and he was guest of honour at a lunch hosted by the Prime Minister at the Savoy in London on 7 March. The papers in the British archives on this important meeting between the Prime Minister and the influential Donovan, fresh from first-hand observation of the Middle East theatre, are not without an amusing aspect. The file begins with a bureaucratic flurry responding to complaints by Churchill about the inferior food and lack of privacy at the Savoy lunch. It seems that the Prime Minister and his guest were forced to discuss these important matters within earshot of another luncheon party with which they had to share the dining room.[207]

British nervousness about the Greek venture continued. The well-placed Colville reported in his diary on 5 March that

> Last night David Margesson told me how much he disliked
> the whole venture upon which we are about to embark. Many
> others feel the same. It was thrust upon us partly because,
> in the first place, the P.M. felt that our prestige in France,
> in Spain and in the U.S. could not stand our desertion of
> Greece; partly because Eden, Dill, Wavell and Cunningham
> recommended it so strongly.[208]

A footnote adds: 'Wavell, having been opposed to the whole scheme of intervention on behalf of Greece, veered round and became its warm exponent.'

Donovan flew home to America on 18 March, travelling on to Washington the following day to report to Secretary Knox and the President. His two journeys to London have been viewed by commentators as significant for wartime Anglo–American relations, and particularly for the impetus and models they provided for the creation of US intelligence organisations: first the COI in June 1941, then the OSS in 1943, and finally the post-war CIA in 1947. Significantly, Roosevelt's creation of the COI, and the appointment of Donovan to the post, were reported to London by the British agent in Washington, William Stephenson, on 18 June 1941 in the following terms:

> Donovan saw President today and . . . accepted appointment.
> He will be co-ordinator of all forms [of] intelligence including
> offensive operations . . . you can imagine how relieved I am
> after three weeks of battle and jockeying for position in
> Washington that *our man* is in such a position of importance
> to our efforts.[209]

Donovan's report on his Mediterranean travels, presented formally to Knox, but in reality prepared for the President himself, was described by the British Ambassador in Madrid, Sir Samuel Hoare, as 'a remarkable document, of the greatest importance'. It began by urging that the President could now have 'a vital and decisive influence on the war'. Then followed the crucial reassurance that

> I have seen that England has done a superb job in this area
> from a strategic, tactical and administrative standpoint. Its

quality can be truly appreciated only by actually seeing that
so much has been done with so little. Now she needs further
aid.

Donovan urged that the Mediterranean be seen not merely as an 'east-
west line of communication, but as a no-man's land between two lines
on a strategic front running from Spain to the Black Sea'. He proposed
that the British be encouraged to enlarge their foothold on the 'northern
line' in Greece, so as to make the Mediterranean an 'interior' rather
than an 'exterior' line of communication. The German aim in Greece
was seen as 'tranquility and security in the Balkans so as to maintain
uninterrupted her supplies of oil, food and raw materials'. Donovan
warned that, unless the British contested Greece,

> Germany might be content for a time to take her gains,
> absorb the Balkans by whatever means, consolidate her
> defences and come to the peace table with most of Europe
> under her dominion, and all the prestige of having withstood
> the mobilisation of the democracies against her ... Her
> defeat cannot be compassed only by economic blockade and
> air bombardment. It is a truism to say that the will of her
> people must be broken and her armies must be at some point
> thrown on the defensive and beaten in the field. The Balkans
> offer perhaps the only place for such a defeat.[210]

On 8 March 1941 the Lend-Lease Bill was passed by Congress,
and on 15 March FDR told White House correspondents: 'The
British people and their Grecian allies need ships. From America
they will get ships. They need planes. From America they will get
planes ... '[211] Bit by bit, the fruits appeared from the carefully
nurtured relationship with the American President, the wooing of
his emissaries, and, we must suspect, the undertaking of a fore-
doomed military adventure in Greece.

On 11 April, the same Good Friday that saw a disconsolate Athens-
bound General Wavell in Flight Lieutenant Frame's Sunderland
T9046 reflecting on military adversity, President Roosevelt sent a
message to Prime Minister Churchill beginning:

> We propose immediately to take the following steps in
> relation to the security of the Western hemisphere, which will
> favourably affect your shipping problem. It is important for
> domestic political reasons which you will readily understand

that this action be taken by us unilaterally and not after diplomatic conversations between you and us. Therefore, before taking this unilateral action I want to tell you about the proposal . . . [212]

Having tipped this very obvious wink, the President detailed the elements of a plan by which America would effectively take over the protection of convoys to the west of a mid-Atlantic line. Further, the Red Sea was to be declared no longer a war zone, with the important consequence that American ships could deliver war *matériel* there without breaching the Neutrality Acts. It seems in fact that the step had been anticipated:

> Actually, American vessels were at that time already en route to Middle Eastern ports. By the end of May forty cargo ships and fifty tankers were assigned to this shuttle service. Thus began the process by which this country [the US] gradually took over the supply of Britain's forces in Egypt.[213]

The measures reported by the President to Churchill on Good Friday thus provided the missing elements to alleviate the British supply problem: American air and sea forces would provide convoy protection on 'their side' of the Atlantic, and American ships could bring war *matériel* through Basra to replenish British forces in the Middle East.

Eight months later, on the evening of Sunday, 7 December 1941, Churchill was dining at Chequers with the American Ambassador, Winant, and Averell Harriman, when he learned first from the radio, and then from President Roosevelt's telephone call, of the Japanese attack on Pearl Harbor. He knew that the long diplomatic courtship was over. Churchill subsequently wrote:

> I knew the United States was in the war, up to the neck and in to the death. So we had won after all! . . . Silly people, and there were many, not only in enemy countries, might discount the force of the United States . . . But I had studied the American Civil War, fought out to the last desperate inch. American blood flowed in my veins. I thought of a remark which Edward Grey had made to me more than thirty years before – that the United States is like 'a gigantic boiler. Once the fire is lighted under it there is no limit to the power it can generate'. Being saturated and satiated with emotion and

sensation, I went to bed and slept the sleep of the saved and
thankful.[214]

Some sense of the extent to which the courtship of American public
opinion and leadership had formed – even *de*formed – British
military planning in the first half of 1941 is evident from Churchill's
reported remark on the day after Pearl Harbor, when he was urged
to have regard to American sensitivities in a proposed message of
support:

> Oh! That is the way we talked to her while we were wooing
> her; now that she is in the harem, we talk to her quite
> differently.[215]

8. Comrades in Arms

Of Henry Lamond I had heard my father speak, in the context both of wartime flying boats and of friendship. I had learned from my subsequent reading in the logbook and elsewhere that Lamond was a New Zealander, born in Kaukapakapa, north of Auckland, and a ubiquitous second-in-command in Alec's Sunderland crew, starting in 1939 with 210 Squadron at Pembroke Dock and continuing with 228 Squadron in the Mediterranean at the end of 1940. The pair had delivered T9046 to Malta, to join 228 Squadron there. The Frame/Lamond team had been broken up only by Lamond's promotion to captaincy duties in his own right in early April 1941, just as rescue operations in Greece were intensifying. I knew that Lamond in T9048 had played an important role in the evacuation flights from Greece, including one flight which carried a record 84 passengers. Also that his Sunderland T9048 had crashed while attempting a difficult night landing without lights in Kalamata Bay on 25 April 1941. Eight of the crew were killed, and the four survivors, including Lamond and Bill Goldfinch, were taken prisoner, both turning their skills to escape plans for the remainder of the war.[216]

On Sunday, 4 May 2003, I drove a rental car from Oxford to the town of Saint Ives, just north of Cambridge. The two-hour journey down the motorway towards London, and back north-eastwards for Cambridge, was relieved only by flashes of bright yellow fields of flowering rape. The 88-year-old Henry Lamond, with a Lloyd George moustache in old age, greeted me outside his unit in a cluster of small but tidy flats, invited me in and sat me down with a cup of tea in a living room comfortably strewn with magazines, presided over by a TV set and pictures of great-grandchildren. The infectious laugh which I had heard on the telephone from London punctuated Henry's talk of growing up around Auckland, his memories of Great Barrier Island and Auckland Grammar School. My sheepish confession of having attended King's College, the great rival school in Auckland, drew more guffaws. Henry's association with a model aeroplane shop in Newmarket and an Auckland gliding club had led to a scholarship to learn to fly, first at Mangere and later at Wigram in the South Island. Spotted as likely material by RAF recruiters, he was selected for travel to the UK for further training and found himself at the flying-boat school at Calshot in early 1939.

Henry talked easily and warmly about my father. The early days at Pembroke Dock in 210 Squadron when they first teamed up – 'Alec did the flying and I did the navigating'. Henry had reported to the squadron from Calshot on 3 October 1939, and the first entry in the logbook citing the Frame/Lamond team was on 8 October 1939, when Sunderland L2163 flew from Pembroke Dock to Oban on the west coast of Scotland. On 10 October they were searching for enemy naval units north of the Faroe Islands on a ten-hour flight. On 17 October, Henry flew solo in a Sunderland, L5800, for the first time. Thereafter, the combination appears regularly in Alec's logbook.

Figure 43: Henry Lamond at Saint Ives, near Cambridge, in England, 4 May 2003.

Henry, dapper and slight; Alec, taller and heavier built. The two 24-year-old New Zealanders were close friends as well as comrades. Henry said that Alec 'liked a pint of beer' and at my request drew a map showing their favourite pub in Tenby, near Pembroke Dock. Once, he said, they had been stood down from duty for 48 hours and had settled in there for a session, when they were unexpectedly recalled to 'PD'. The local police were apparently very helpful in getting the two legless flyers back to base, where their batmen administered cold baths before they presented themselves for duty. Their Sunderland soon wove its way through the channels and sand-bars of Milford Haven towards deeper water. 'Take-off out of Angle Bay was pretty rough', Henry added, wincing. Alec was certainly an enthusiastic drinker in his day, although in civilian life he had a strict rule of 'no drink the day before flying'. As a boy I remember his rigid observance of this in the face of strenuous urgings of the 'just one' type from well-meaning drinking companions.

Henry had a high regard for Alec's flying skills, mentioning that 'he was a past master at flying up the Caledonian Canal', the diagonal gash, surrounded by hills, between Oban on the west coast of Scotland and Invergordon on the east. Henry had written to me before our meeting in England:

> We had 4 pilots to a Sunderland crew before we had navigators and the plan was to do two hours first pilot, two hours as second pilot, two hours as navigator and two hours off in which we went to sleep on the bunk in the downstairs wardroom. But your father was always captain and seldom got out of the left-hand pilot's seat as I remember.[217]

Henry also recalled Alec's development of a technique for taking off a Sunderland on three engines: it consisted of starting down wind and allowing speed to build up until the uneven thrust brought the boat around 180 degrees into the wind and up on to the step.

The delivery flight of T9046 to Malta in December 1940 has already been recounted in Chapter 5. On 4 December Alec and Henry flew the new Mark I Sunderland from Mount Batten to Gibraltar. The logbook declares that the flight took ten hours – five of them at night, no doubt to reduce the risk of interception by German fighters in the Bay of Biscay – and that there were two passengers, Group Captain Pelly and Dr Atkinson. Henry told me that the take-off from Mount Batten was difficult: not only was a heavy fuel load required for the long flight, but a spare Pegasus engine had been stowed aboard. Henry looked at me with a twinkle in his eye. 'They put it right above our whisky hideaway so we couldn't get at it!' he said, adding more seriously that they got off Plymouth Sound only at the third try.

The arrival of T9046 in Malta on 6 December marked the beginning of an exciting period for the two New Zealanders. For Alec, the depression of Oamaru and the dreary peace-time routines of army life at Trentham were far behind. Now, at the top of his game as a Sunderland pilot, and already a seasoned commander of men in war, he was breathing the oxygen of new experience mixed with the adrenalin of danger. All of this was intensified and stabilised by the camaraderie and *esprit de corps* of the officers' mess. The disturbing truth may be that this was the high time of my father's life.

The Frame/Lamond partnership would see much action before Henry took up command in his own right of Sunderland T9048, just in time to play an important role in 228 Squadron's contribution to the evacuations from Greece. As we have seen, however, this ended in tragedy when, on the night of 25 April 1941, T9048 crashed while attempting an unlit night landing at Kalamata.

John Whelan begins his account of Lamond's activities on that day with this explanation:

> Flight-Lieutenant H.W. Lamond was detailed to search for a party in the Githeon area in Greece. At Githeon Greek officers in laboured French directed him to a bay farther south-west, where the crew observed flashes from a hand mirror and picked up 52 officers and men of a Royal Air Force fighter squadron. Lamond returned immediately to evacuate a party which Frame had noted near Kalamata. He took aboard 72 men waiting in the harbour area. This still stands as the record number of passengers ever carried in a flight by a Sunderland. Lamond carefully disposed his passengers to balance the aircraft, firmly preventing anyone, irrespective of rank, from bringing aboard any luggage or personal effects. Carrying only 400 gallons of petrol, the Sunderland finally became airborne after ricocheting off the harbour.[218]

Whelan continues with an account of the crash at Kalamata:

> The same evening at eleven o'clock Lamond returned to Kalamata to deliver a message to a senior officer of the remaining air force personnel. The take-off had been made

Figure 44: Kalamata seafront in 2005. The Sunderlands boarded their passengers here, and two days later Jack Hinton won the VC in a grenade rampage beginning along the street behind.

> without a flare path and there was none available for the landing, which was attempted by the use of the aircraft's landing light on a glassy and deceptive surface. The pilot found it practically impossible to judge his height, and the aircraft hit the sea heavily and broke up. Lamond and three of his crew were the only survivors. A portion of the hull remained afloat, and on this the four stayed until Lamond's shouts attracted the attention of a small Greek fishing boat . . . Three of the aircrew, including Flight Lieutenant Lamond, were taken to a military hospital where they later became prisoners of war. For his share in the evacuation Lamond was awarded the Greek Distinguished Flying Cross.[219]

I was worried about raising the Kalamata crash with Henry on my visit in May 2003. My father had not talked about it, and I had learned of it only through historical accounts.[220] I sensed that there were 'issues' here: the loss of comrades, the strange phenomenon of 'survivor guilt', the disturbing effect of lengthy imprisonment by the enemy, and the inevitable quest for explanations and reasons. I asked Henry directly whether he was comfortable discussing the

Reports had been received from aircraft T9046 that a large party of R.A.F.
personnel were in the KALAMATA area:so T 9048 F/Lt Lamond was ordered to
this area instead of returning to Githeon: At Kalamata the R.A.F; party
was waiting in the Harbour area. 72 members of the party were take aboard
This is a record number of passengers ever carried during a flight by a
Sunderland. This large number was arranged is such a way that the stability of the aircraft was not affected: No bombs were carried and only
350-400 gallons of petrol was aboard. The take off was not excessively
long even shorter than the usual run with full military load.

On returning to Suda Bay T 9048 was at first ordered to refuel to 1800
gallonsprior to taking off the next morning on a patrol. However a message was
was flashed from the shore to refuel to 700 gallons only and to return that
night to KALAMATA to deliver a message from the A.O.C.R.A.F. Greece to
Group Captain Lee. The take off was made without flare path. At approximately 2330 the aircraft was over the Harbour of Kalamata; As gthere
was no flare path available the landing was made by Landing Light. The
conditions of the seawas calm; On landing the aircraft crashed and broke
up immediately: Four members of the crew ?The Captain F/Lt Lamond, P/O
Goldfinch, P/O Briscoe and Sergeant Davis were the only survivors.
          A portion of the hull remained afloat and in this the
four members remained until the calls for help given by F/Lt Lamond attracted the attention of a small Greek fishing boat.The search part from the
shore had failed to locate the wreck and had given up the search.
          F/Lt Lamond, P/O Goldfinch and Sergeant Davis were taken
to the Kalamata Military Hospital whilst P/O Briscoe was taken to a local
Nursing Home
          It is feared that the remainder of the crew F/O Lylian,
P/O Lynton, Sergeant Cooper, Sergeant James, Sergeant Warren and L.A.C
Summers lost their lives in the crash.
          It is believed that F/Lt Lamond, P/O Goldfinch and Sergeant
Davis have Ballen into enemy hands and have been made Prisoners of War.
          P/O Briscoe was evacuated with the R.A.F. party under
Group Captain Lee.

Figure 45: Excerpt from 228 Squadron ORB recording the crash of T9048 at Kalamata on 25 April 1941.

matter. To my surprise and relief, he said that he *wanted* to discuss it. What was more, after Henry's liberation at the end of the war, my father had been best man at his wedding on 4 August 1945, and the two men had discussed the events and were in agreement on the issues.

The two Sunderlands, T9046 and T9048, were moored in Suda Bay in Crete on the night of 25 April with the crews asleep, exhausted from the evacuation missions of the previous days. By my count, Alec had flown twelve sorties in the previous four days and Henry had already flown four sorties that day alone. The commander of the group made up of 228 and 230 Squadrons sent instructions directly to Henry on T9048 to take off immediately for Kalamata with a message from Air Vice-Marshal d'Albiac for Group Captain A.G. Lee to the effect that no further ships could be sent for the evacuation. Henry quickly readied for departure, taxied out into the bay, and took off in the dark – he remembered seeing 'the sunken ship masts sticking out of the water'. Kalamata, an hour and a half away, was in darkness and the Sunderland attempted an unlit landing on a 'flat calm' surface. The altimeter was showing 300 feet when the aircraft struck the water.

In his letter to me, which I received on my return to New Zealand, Henry wrote:

> I should have woken him [Alec] up that night I crashed a Sunderland trying to do a night-landing without a flare path at a harbour in Greece. He had already proved that he could do it by doing a night-landing without a flare path somewhere along the coast of North Africa when we were operating from Malta. I had to spend 4 years and 4 days as a POW.[221]

Henry said that Alec's view was that he was entitled, as the senior 228 Squadron officer on the spot, to be consulted about the order and would have discussed the feasibility of the mission, and the question of who should fly it, with the commanding officer. The suggestion is that Alec would have either advised against the mission or insisted on flying it himself, with his much greater flying experience, particularly of night landings. I have come to wonder whether, hidden behind the sheer exhaustion and 'fog of war', a certain blurring of chains of command was created by the *de facto* merging of 228 and 230 Squadrons at Alexandria as the crews and serviceable aircraft were depleted. After the departure of Nicholetts as 228 Squadron's leader, the hitherto nominal and administrative role of '210 Group' seems to have become more formal and led to some confusion and resentment.

After my return to New Zealand, I found in Archives New Zealand in Wellington a letter written in 1950 by Henry Lamond to an official New Zealand war historian in which he describes the Kalamata events. He states that he could not recall the details of the message he was sent to Kalamata to deliver but that

> . . . it was quite an urgent requirement as it meant night flying for the whole operation without the usual essential facility of a flare path either at Suda Bay or at Kalamata . . . On arriving and identifying Kalamata Bay I attempted a landing but the water was too calm for my aircraft landing light to be effective and I crashed. The controls were wrenched from my hands on impact and the aircraft turned over.[222]

After the crash, the unconscious survivors were treated by Greek medical staff. Henry had been thrown through the windscreen of T9048 on impact and was cut around the head and face. Bill Goldfinch said that he looked terrible but mended remarkably quickly in the care of the medical staff and nurses in the Greek military hospital at Kalamata.

Henry subsequently endured great hardship as he made his way by forced march and cattle truck to prison camp in Germany. In April 1942 Henry and two other RAF officers dug their way under the wire of the Luftwaffe's new prison for air force crew at Sagan; they were recaptured five days later near Stettin.[223]

Figure 46: Flight Lieutenant Henry Lamond's T9048 boarding RAF evacuees in Kalamata Bay during the day of 24 April 1941. The location is verified by the background, which includes the village of Vergas on the hill to the right. Bill Goldfinch identified himself, third from left in the photograph, in the high flying-boots which provided such poor protection on the march into German captivity after the disaster that night.

Henry's views on the command and conduct of the British forces at Kalamata are very unflattering. He told me, and repeated when I queried the strength of his comment, that 'the British officers didn't know how to fight and didn't know how to look after their troops'. He thought that the 22,000 men concentrated at Kalamata, access to which was by a single and eminently defensible road, ought to have been able to hold off, for the time required to organise evacuation, the 'handful of Germans' available to attack the town and command the port. Indeed, he pointed to the action of Sergeant J.D. Hinton of New Zealand's 20 Battalion, who counter-attacked with a dozen men and drove the German attackers from the quay area, so earning the only VC awarded for the campaign in Greece.[224] Henry said that the British military authorities held an inquiry after the war into whether a proper defence had been conducted.

Lieutenant E.H. Simpson of 22 Battalion, New Zealand Division, signed an account of the surrender at Kalamata as he was evacuated on the ship *Isis* on 30 April:

> We learnt that Brigadier Parrington had ordered the men to lay down their arms at 0500, 29th April as he considered they were short of food and ammunition. It is unfortunate that his information was incorrect, on both these points.[225]

Figure 47: Kalamata Bay in 2005. The village of Vergas can be seen on the slopes to the right.

Here I think we see the emergence of a certain friction between 'Dominion' and 'British' officers and fighting men. The matter seems well expressed by Freyberg's personal assistant, John White:

It takes time for men from the Dominions and men from the old country to learn how to work together. To us they appear haphazard, lacking in system – their hours for meals, their dress, their 'old boy, old school tie, cum Poona' language, their caste system – take a bit of getting used to, while for him the lack of these things, the brusqueness and disregard of the formalities in men from the Dominions is so galling at first that we are likely to have the honour of being classed as 'socially impossible'.[226]

Henry had not been aware of my father's death 20 years before. They had lost contact when Alec went to Tahiti. He shook his head, saying: 'I can't believe it. I should have been dead 60 years ago and here I am alive. Alec was the strong man for me, and he's been dead for 20 years.' Henry asked what route I planned to take on the drive back to Oxford and, dissatisfied with my vague reply, pulled out maps on the dining-room table and started plotting me a course. I regret to say that I later became hopelessly lost on country roads and found myself spending the night in a motel in Hatfield, right by the site of the old De Havilland Flying School, where Alec had his first flying lessons in January 1938.

After my visit to Henry Lamond, I travelled by train to Salisbury, the home of Bill Goldfinch, another of Alec's comrades from 228 Squadron and a survivor of the Kalamata crash in 1941. At 87, Bill Goldfinch was a well-preserved, gently courteous and thoughtful Englishman, tallish and slender. A famous man, too, for he played the principal role in the design and construction of the 'Colditz glider' built to carry prisoners to freedom from the German fortress prison. I had written to him from New Zealand, enclosing copies of some pages from Alec's logbook for the period January–June 1941 and drawing attention to the entry for 13 February, recording my father's command of the unaccustomed Sunderland L2164 on a ten-hour patrol over the Ionian Sea, with Pilot Officer Goldfinch also on the flight deck. At the National Archives in Kew, I had seen Bill's name in the 228 Squadron ORB. He had arrived in Malta in a batch of six new pilots from the No 20 Flying Training School in Rhodesia in early February 1941. He was in Squadron Leader Nicholetts's crew a month later when Sunderland L5807 flew the American 'Wild Bill' Donovan and Admiral Lyster, the planner of the successful attack on the Italian fleet in Taranto harbour in November 1940, from Malta to Gibraltar and on to Mount Batten.

Bill Goldfinch picked me up from my hotel in Salisbury and we drove to the nearby Old Sarum airfield. This decommissioned RAF base is situated at the foot of a mound of ancient earthworks which a thousand years ago supported a cathedral, castle, and keep, the precursor of the subsequent city of Salisbury. The drill and order of military aviation had given way to a gaudy but interesting assortment of private aircraft, and the tarmac was a colourful cluster of light planes and the increasingly popular micro-lights. Bill was clearly well known here and we stopped frequently to return greetings as we made our way towards one of the hangars. In it were two things Bill wanted to show me. First, the 'Jodel', a single-engined aircraft which Bill had built and flown until he could no longer satisfy the licence requirements – at the age of 85. Second, alongside the Jodel was an emerging construction of fuselage, spars, and a float. Brandishing a roll of plans, Bill introduced his amphibian under construction. Indeed, he soon had me at work on it under his careful guidance.

Figure 48: Bill Goldfinch with plans and aircraft under construction, Old Sarum airfield, near Salisbury, England, 7 May 2003.

Bill remembers the Kalamata crash on the approach – 'dark, no stars, calm' – at about 90 knots, with 300 feet showing on the altimeter. Flying Officer Lylian[227] had his head out the window trying to help Henry Lamond find the water surface. Strangely, the last thing Bill remembers is putting a piece of bread in his mouth. Then blank.

Bill pointed out that, a month after the Kalamata crash, another Sunderland, flown by Vic Hodgkinson, crashed in the Atlantic while trying to put down short of fuel. There, too, the pilot thought he had height but hit the water.[228] Bill believes that training for letting down Sunderlands without visual contact with the water was developed later in the war, but had not at that time been provided for.

Henry Lamond, with whom Bill still had contact, had told me of the long walk the prisoners underwent on the journey from Greece to Germany. Bill suffered particularly because he had only flying boots, which were unsuitable for the rough terrain. Henry had said to 'ask Bill if he remembers the time his feet were so bloody that he had to cover them with earth to keep the blood-sucking insects away'.

Bill dates his interest in escaping from this time. He saw a prisoner in a walking column seize an opportunity to duck out into a culvert, and it set him thinking. The historian of Colditz prison, Henry Chancellor, has chronicled the result, stating that Goldfinch

> . . . had spent his life in captivity dreaming up various flying escapes. At Biberach, a large hutted camp twenty miles from the Swiss border, he had imagined constructing a large biplane kite, which with the aid of a strong wind and a rope would have floated an escaper over the wire and into the woods beyond. At Stalag Luft 3 he had adapted this concept into a gyroplane, but realising the practical difficulties it entailed he had decided to escape by 'moling' under the perimeter fence with Jack Best. They were caught, and it was only when Goldfinch arrived at Colditz that his flying ideas gained credibility.[229]

The result was the 'Colditz glider', built by a team – Bill was quick to insist on this point – in a space created by a false wall. It was to have carried two men out of the castle and over the walls and was practically ready when Colditz was liberated by Allied forces in 1945. Chancellor writes: 'Bill Goldfinch's working drawings were meticulous; the glider required over six thousand pieces of wood, each of a specific length and width, and many of them no bigger than a matchstick.'

As we finished up for the day on the amphibian, I ventured to ask Bill what he would do with the aircraft when it was complete, given that he no longer had a licence to fly. He looked at me with a twinkle in his eye: 'Oh, fast taxiing,' he said innocently.

Over tea in the cafeteria we looked at pictures I had brought with me. Bill solved one puzzle immediately: after Henry Lamond's promotion to command, his place was taken in the logbook by Pilot Officer J.C. Paré. I had not been able to find any background on this officer, who was often on the flight deck of T9046 during the evacuations from Greece and Crete. Bill pointed out Paré as a tall figure in the passing-out picture at No 20 Flying Training School in Rhodesia; he arrived at 228 Squadron in Malta on the same day as Bill in February 1941.[230] We were then joined for a time by a cheerful Australian mechanic working at the airfield, Peter Smith, who had served as bowman on the only surviving airworthy Sunderland-variant, and written a book about it.[231] Peter kindly helped me to understand some technical aspects of mooring equipment. Later, Bill drove me back to my hotel and, on learning that I planned to visit Greece, asked if I would try to thank the staff at Kalamata for the care given to the four T9048 survivors.

Two years later, in April 2005, my Singapore Airlines Boeing 777 flew more than six miles high up the Persian Gulf towards Basra before turning west along the border between Saudi Arabia and Iraq to enter the Mediterranean near Beirut. Soon, the sun rose behind as the aircraft crossed Cyprus and began the descent towards Athens, so beginning my visit to Kalamata hoping to find more information on the Sunderland evacuations in 1941. I took with me a photograph said to show '230 Squadron aircraft during the evacuation from Crete'. Two days later I showed it to Yannis at the desk of the Akti Taigetos Hotel just out of Kalamata. He immediately identified the background. 'That is my village,' he said with certainty, pointing at the buildings clustered in the fold of the hill face to the right: 'Vergas'. Further inquiry established without doubt that the photograph is of Henry Lamond's 228 Squadron Sunderland T9048 in Kalamata Bay during the day of 24 April 1941.

Later, I showed the picture to a pretty young librarian at the Kalamata public library in the city centre, hoping to discover the names of the fishermen who had rescued the survivors of T9048 from the waters of the bay. Originals of the Kalamata newspaper *Tharos* for the days of 26 and 27 April 1941 were soon produced. Naturally, the news was all of the German advance into Greece on all fronts, but there was nothing on the Sunderland crash. The librarian frowned. 'My father knows about these things – I will call him.'

Her father was Niko Zervis, the leading scholar on the history of Kalamata during the war, and the author of several books on the subject. This charming and generous man, who had been a teenager in Kalamata at the time and whose father had survived a Nazi concentration camp, came to meet me at the library. His interests stretched beyond the military aspects: he knew Lawrence Durrell and had also published a book on that writer's connection with Kalamata in 1941. Later that day, Niko sent me copies of his books. As we parted on the street outside the library, and remembering Bill Goldfinch's request, I asked him where the military hospital had been in 1941. With a smile he pointed to the building next to the library from which we had just emerged on Aristomenous Street. It was no longer a hospital, of course, and there was no nursing staff to thank on Bill's behalf. But that night I watched the light fade over Kalamata Bay. Somewhere out there, just after midnight on 25 April 1941, Henry Lamond, John Lylian, Bill Goldfinch, and the crew of T9048 groped for the glassy surface, and found it too suddenly.

9. Despair in Crete

The diary of Sergeant James Pickett of the New Zealand Artillery helped us in Chapter 6 to see the essential features of the retreat in Greece as they appeared to the common soldier. Now, the same brief chronicle will summarise the agony in Crete a month later and its tragic ending, both for the diarist and for the British, New Zealand, and Australian force of which his unit formed part under the command of his compatriot, General Freyberg. The little pocket-book takes us to the first day of the German airborne assault on the island:

> *Tuesday 20 May* – The big stink. This is hell. Even as I write the planes. Never seen so many in all my life. Hundreds. Many killed.
> *Friday 23 May* – This is the 4th day. How long will it keep up? No sleep.
> *Saturday 24 May* – Counter attack. No sleep. Lay down at 4.20 am but too much noise. Had a talk with God and feel much better.
> *Sunday 25 May* – First sight of RAF – 6 [illegible] 6 Hurricanes bombed drome – usual strafing and mortar barrage. I can take it now. Not scared any more. Many happies Annette.[232]

James Pickett, whose religion is given as Methodist, was killed later that Sunday – within a short time of making the final entry, the last words of which are a reference to a relative or friend whose name appears in a list of birthdays at the front of the diary. He was 21. The diary came to the Alexander Turnbull Library in Wellington, New Zealand, from the Commonwealth War Graves Commission to which it had been sent by its German counterpart in 1987, that organisation having been given it by the widow of a German veteran of the battle for Crete. Some small photographs were with the diary: strangely, one was of a group of airmen in Greece with a significance soon to appear.

Another startled New Zealand soldier on 20 May was Major J.K. Elliott of Wellington, a surgeon attached to Freyberg's Creforce headquarters, who wrote:

> On the 20th the Huns were over at daylight. At about 8 am someone yelled 'Christ, come and look at this!'. I ducked up the bank behind our office tent and saw one of the most astonishing sights I have ever seen. Big slow black heavy-bodied JU 52 troop carriers were coming over in numbers too big to count. They were dropping parachutists. [233]

In 2003, my arrival in Crete from Alexandria via Athens did not augur well. Delay everywhere and I was short of sleep. Heraklion airport was full of German jetliners disgorging thousands of affluent-looking tourists – could these grandfathers also be here to remember the events of 62 years ago? My taxi-driver from the airport spoke German and seemed disappointed that I did not. Having settled a price at the start, he tried to increase it on arrival at the hotel. Then I found that the hotel charged extra for turning on the air-conditioning in the room. This was not promising.

Figure 49: Suda Bay from the War Cemetery in 2003 – an alley of naval and aerial warfare and destruction in May 1941.

Next day I set off by the trusty KTEL state-owned bus system for Chania, where I had hoped to link up with the commemorative events, details of which the helpful New Zealand Consul-General in Athens, Costas Cotsilinis, had given me. My preparation for this last leg of my journey had not been as careful as for earlier stages and I now found that Crete was much bigger than I had anticipated – there was no possibility of skipping whimsically up and down the island in pursuit of the 1941 story. Then I found that I was well off track for the commemorative events, which were more widely scattered than I had imagined. And my inability to speak any Greek was proving more of a handicap than I had foreseen. My bus rolled westwards along the northern coast of Crete . . .

Enter Manousos. By chance, in Chania, wondering quite how I could salvage something from this visit to Crete, I hailed a taxi – a blue Mercedes Benz. At the wheel was a confident young man with a nice smile and, I quickly learned, good English. I explained that I wanted to get to the service that evening at Suda Bay War Cemetery. Yes, this could be done, he said, and, as we drove, he introduced himself and questioned me further about my reasons for being in Crete. On learning of the background, Manousos proclaimed that his grandfather, killed by the Germans in 1941, and my father had fought side by side against the common enemy. Furthermore, Sphakia, on the south coast, the village from which the final evacuations were made and which I wanted to visit, was his home village. Manousos found me a hotel in Suda Bay and arranged to pick me up on the following day for the journey across the mountains to Sphakia.

Later in the afternoon I walked the three miles from the town to the Allied war cemetery at the head of the long and sheltered Suda Bay – dubbed 'bomb alley' by the defending forces in 1941. Sheltered by the hills on either side and by olive groves inland, the rows of white stones slope gently towards the placid bay across the well-tended grass. Here, on Saturday, 24 May 2003, British, Australian, and New Zealand contingents of veterans and officials, and representatives of their Greek and Cretan allies, were gathering for the 62nd commemoration of the battle and of the lives lost. As the sun set behind us, the New Zealand Foreign Minister, Phil Goff, laid a wreath on behalf of the New Zealand Government.

From this bay Alec flew T9046 seven times during April and May 1941. He brought Air Marshal Longmore here from Cairo on 22 April – the day the evacuation from Greece began – to assess the possibility of providing effective fighter defence for the island when the forces withdrawing from Greece arrived there. Longmore duly reported that 'There should be a reasonable chance of keeping Suda Bay usable by the Navy by one Hurricane Squadron with 100 per cent reserve pilots and replacement rate 100 per cent per month . . . '[234]

Figure 50: Suda Bay Commonwealth War Graves, 24 May 2003. A piper opens the commemoration service on the 62nd anniversary of the battle for Crete.

Suda Bay, with its forest of funnels and masts of ships sunk by air attack and by one bold foray by Italian torpedo boats, was the staging-post for 228 and 230 Squadrons' evacuation flights from Greece. Alec's T9046, and T9048 with Henry Lamond and Bill Goldfinch and John Lylian and the others, had moored together here for the last time before the Kalamata crash on 25 April 1941.

The commemorative event was organised by the British Embassy in Athens, and a British Anglican minister led the service. Unfortunately, the Greek band and the Anglican minister could not synchronise the singing of the first hymn, which fell apart embarrassingly, the band being finally waved to silence. But the ceremony was still moving, and Phil Goff read a well-chosen biblical text in a firm tone. Afterwards, in the dusk, I walked around the New Zealand section of the cemetery, seeing names I recognised: Takarangi and Vercoe and Kyle. All together here, Maori and Pakeha. I found myself calling to them quietly:

> Tena ra koutou nga tino toa o Aotearoa,
> Maori Pakeha hoki – tena koutou katoa.
> Ahakoa e takoto nei o koutou tupapaku
> Ki tenei whenua – o Kiriti,
> Kua rere atu o koutou rongonui
> Ki nga marae maha o Aotearoa.[235]

Next morning, Manousos and the blue Mercedes appeared at the appointed hour and we set off, soon beginning the climb into the central mountains of Crete. This was the route for the tired and numb Allied troops in the last week of May 1941 as they and their officers sought to escape to the south coast and the promise of ships to take them to Egypt. It was longer, steeper, and rougher than I had supposed and I congratulated myself on having abandoned an initial plan to attempt even part of the route on foot. We came to the highest plateau and the village of Imros, where the mother of Manousos had a house. Then we began the descent towards the coast of Sphakia and the village itself, Hora Sphakia. Several hairpin bends in the road reminded me of Evelyn Waugh's description of the scene in 1941:

> After Imvros the road ended in a series of exposed hairpin bends. A track to the left diverged and ran through the gorge to the coast; between the mouth of the gorge and the foot of the road was a village and another small gorge; then an open rump of hillside and a further gorge, full of caves, which led down to Sphakia, the port of embarkation . . . [236]

In Hora Sphakia, Manousos was well received, as was his explanation for my visit. An old fisherman, Giannis Tzardis, talked to us while stowing his nets in his fishing boat. He had been fifteen years old in 1941 and witnessed the chaos of the evacuation. He pointed out places where embarkation for the waiting ships took place. He remembered that 'only English' soldiers were allowed on the *Glen Earn*, and that New Zealanders and Australians were turned away. He had not heard of, or seen, any flying boats.

A little later, I had a swim in the clear water nearby and, putting my notebook away, began to think about lunch. But Manousos had become a task-master: 'I feel we have more to learn here,' he said sternly. Just then, two pale old men made their way towards us and, in the exaggerated monotone adopted by those not expecting to be understood, one said: 'Do-you-know-where-Harbour-Master?' Manousos and I looked blankly at each other. 'We-were-here-in-19-41,' the man went on ploddingly. Manousos smiled at me triumphantly and said, 'Now, you talk.'

Figure 51: Wearing hats, Jack Baker and Johnny Vellacott, 30 Squadron veterans of Greece and Crete. On right, the author's driver and guide, Manousos. Taken in Sphakia, Crete, on 24 May 2003.

These were two RAF 30 Squadron men, Johnny Vellacott and Jack Baker, who had been evacuated first from Greece and then from Sphakia. They had been at the Suda Bay cemetery the evening before, and now wanted verification of the embarkation points on the beach here – hence their hopeless quest for the 'harbour-master'. Although both men were taken off by ship, Jack Baker told me that he had been flown by Sunderland from Scaramanga in Greece to Suda Bay on 24 April. A quick check in the logbook showed that Alec had flown T9046 from Scaramanga to Suda Bay that day with '40 RAF passengers'. It seemed very likely that one of these was Jack. I showed the men the passenger list for T9046 from Sphakia on the night of 30 May, and with obvious emotion they recognised the names of comrades from 30 Squadron. Manousos beamed at us.

In 1987 the widow of a German paratrooper gave to the German equivalent of the War Graves Commission items from her husband's papers. As explained earlier, these have found their way to the Alexander Turnbull Library in Wellington. The first item was the diary of Sergeant James Pickett, who was killed in action on Crete on 25 May 1941. A second item is a group of eighteen photographs, with captions, of RAF pilots and some Blenheim aircraft. One of the captions identifies three pilots, W.K. Branch, D.J. Vellacott, and G.W. Ratlidge. Names featuring in captions for other photographs are 'Maxy' Welsh, 'Doc' Ferguson, J.A.F. Attwell, Cartwrigh?[t], Sergeant Tony Ovens, Sergeant H. Lord, 'Twiggy' Branch, and Flight Sergeant D.J. Innes-Smith. Some pictures have no captions and are of aircraft and tents.

I did not become aware of these records until my return to New Zealand, but it is clear to me that the eighteen photographs, in excellent condition, are of 30 Squadron personnel. It seems also that the photographs and Sergeant Pickett's diary are not related, except that they both somehow fell into the hands of a German paratrooper on Crete (perhaps at the fighting around Maleme airfield) and have come to be seen as a single item.[237]

Later, as we left Hora Sphakia, Manousos stopped the Mercedes at a whitewashed concrete enclosure with a rusting wrought-iron cage-like construction in the centre. I followed him in and soon saw that the cage contained bleached human skulls and bones – an ossuary. These were the remains of the Cretan resistance fighters and hostages shot by the Germans for assisting General Freyberg's forces. Among them, Manousos's grandfather.

On our way back across the mountains, Manousos stopped at Imros where his relatives had a restaurant. We were served three kinds of lamb and some 'wild grass' (rather like our New Zealand puha) and a fine local wine, for which our hosts refused to accept payment. We also visited George Hatzidakis's war museum nearby. An extensive collection of German and Allied war material of all sorts is exhibited there, and knowledgeably explained by the host over a *raki* or two.

Evelyn Waugh's eye-witness account of the battle and evacuation of Crete paints an almost wholly unfavourable picture of the defensive effort. Chaos, confusion, incompetent command, and even cowardice, are the principal features discerned by that commentator, who, it must immediately be conceded, was on the spot.[238] Waugh had joined 8 Commando under Lieutenant Colonel Laycock and at the beginning of December 1940 started training on the island of Arran in preparation for the attack, advocated by Churchill but later cancelled, on the island of Pantelleria. His account of incompetence and pervasive drunkenness in the unit suggests another dimension of 'the fog of war'. Waugh reached Suez on 6 March 1941. Layforce, as Laycock's commando unit was officially named, arrived on Crete to reinforce the garrison, commanded by General Freyberg, on 26 May – the battle by then being effectively over. Indeed, Layforce might have been better named Lateforce. Waugh accompanied Laycock as his intelligence officer.

On Crete, Waugh was appalled by what he saw as the incompetent and shirking attitude of some of the defenders – mainly, but not only, in Layforce itself. One of the few units to be commended by Waugh is the Maori Battalion. The famed Australian self-reliance is given a different aspect:

> All the caves were full of ragged, starving, neurotic Australians who had run away earlier. Whenever an aeroplane was heard, often when it was not, they shouted, 'Aircraft, take cover!' and shot at anyone who moved about. One could hear the wail being passed from cave to cave down the gorge. Some of them had Cretan women living with them in the caves; at night these men sallied forth to raid ration dumps. Some were starving but some had large stores of food they stole in this way. [239]

But Waugh reserves particular criticism for a renamed Colonel 'Hound' of his own British unit, who is described as 'hunched up like a disconsolate ape' under a table and as lying 'rigid with his face in the gorse for about four hours. If anyone stretched a leg, he groaned as though he had broken all his limbs and was being jolted. "For Christ's sake keep still".'[240]

At Sphakia, where the defending forces were concentrating for evacuation, 'Bob' Laycock and Waugh sought out Freyberg's headquarters:

> We found Freyberg just as it was getting dark. He was sitting outside his cave surrounded by miscellaneous staff officers, saying goodbye to New Zealanders who were leaving that

evening. Some had photographs of him which he signed. He gave us half a cupful of sherry and a spoonful of beans for which we were very grateful. He seemed to have lost all interest in the battle, spoke of his earlier successes against the parachute landing in the East with satisfaction. Bob asked him about our order of embarkation and he said: 'You were the last to come so you will be the last to go.'[241]

That night, Laycock and Waugh heard the embarkation going on at Sphakia:

The sailors made a prodigious noise; at the end they were shouting, 'Any more for the boats?' for they could have taken off some hundreds more than they did, had the embarkation been better organized.[242]

Next day:

In the afternoon, the 31st of May, Bob and I went to get further orders and find a place for headquarters. Freyberg had gone but [General] Weston had set up in his cave. The wireless was no longer working. Its last order had been that that night was the last night for evacuation . . .

The painful matter of surrender of the remaining forces on the island now had to be faced. Weston dictated a capitulation to be handed in at dawn the next day:

He first charged Bob with the task but later realised that it was foolish to sacrifice a first-class man for this and chose instead Hound, who had lately attached himself to brigade HQ, where he was a nuisance owing to his having thrown away his water bottle in his flight . . . [243]

A footnote adds: 'Colonel "Hound" then disappeared. The capitulation was effected by Colonel Young.'

Waugh added to this eye-witness report a fictional treatment of the battle for Crete in his novel *Officers and Gentlemen*, first published in 1955. The novel traces the progress of Guy Crouchback and his commando unit from training on the 'Isle of Mugg' to the Middle East and eventually to a belated participation in what we are invited to see as an inglorious debacle in Crete. Crouchback is made to experience the evacuation as a resignation of 'an immeasurable part of his manhood'. Frank Kermode suggests in his introduction to the Everyman's Library edition that Waugh might here have been working off some personal guilt, as his own embarkation on the destroyer *Nizam* appears on its face to have been inconsistent with General Freyberg's specific orders that Layforce, as the last defenders to arrive, should be the last to leave Crete.

> On 31 May, Guy sat in a cave overhanging the beach of Sphakia where the final embarkation was shortly to begin. By his watch it was not yet ten o'clock but it seemed the dead of night. Nothing stirred in the moonlight. In the crowded ravine below the Second Halberdiers stood in column of companies, every man in full marching order, waiting for the boats . . . [244]

Waugh creates a discussion between officers about whether Freyberg's priorities might be disregarded:

> 'The General's off in a flying-boat tonight.'
> 'No staying with the sinking ship.'
> 'Napoleon didn't stay with his army after Moscow.'
> Presently Ivor said: 'What does one *do* in prison?'

The New Zealand scholar, journalist, and soldier Geoffrey Cox was on Freyberg's staff in Crete and ideally placed to write his careful and calm account of the battle and assessment of the reasons for its outcome. Cox was evacuated from Sphakia on the Australian ship *Perth* and states: 'We took a muster roll of the men crowded on the decks below. Among them were a number from the Commando units which were supposed to be forming the rearguard.'[245]

Next day in Hora Sphakia, according to Waugh:

> The golden dawn was changing to unclouded blue. Guy led his section down the rough path to the harbour. The quay was littered with abandoned equipment and the wreckage of bombardment . . . .The little town was burned, battered and deserted by its inhabitants. The ghosts of an army teemed everywhere. Some were quite apathetic, too weary to eat; others were smashing their rifles on the stones, taking a fierce relish in this symbolic farewell to their arms; an officer stamped on his binoculars; a motor bicycle was burning; there was a small group under command of a sapper Captain doing something to a seedy-looking fishing-boat that lay on

its side, out of the water; on the beach. One man sat on the sea-wall methodically stripping down his Bren and throwing the parts separately far into the scum . . . [246]

The New Zealand Prime Minister, Peter Fraser, on his way to London to attend the War Cabinet, had arrived in Egypt just in time for the calamity of Crete. Fraser landed in Cairo on 17 May 1941 after a multi-stage journey from New Zealand – mainly by flying boat – and quickly involved himself in the affairs of the New Zealand Division, visiting the men and conferring with their commanders, including General Wavell.

Alarmingly for the local military command, the Prime Minister immediately expressed a desire to fly to Crete to confer with Freyberg. A secret message for Freyberg on 17 May suggested that Longmore 'might send in a Sunderland during darkness' for the purpose. Freyberg's reaction to this addition to his problems might be imagined: he sent a frantic return message advising against it, citing the 'unique risk of landing aeroplanes'.[247] The last thing General Freyberg needed as he prepared for the onslaught was his Prime Minister to worry about.

On 26 May, two shocks awaited the New Zealand leader. First, General Freyberg announced to Wavell that the military situation on Crete was beyond salvation. Second, in the evening, the Prime Minister and his party were driving back to Cairo from meeting wounded New Zealanders in Alexandria when, at 9.50, a burst tyre caused the car to somersault four times. Serious injuries were sustained by some members of the party, although the Prime Minister suffered only bruises and scratches.[248] 'That's that', Fraser is reported as saying as he picked himself up out of the wreckage.[249]

On 29 May Wavell bluntly signalled to Freyberg, no doubt recalling the latter's disobedience of his instruction to leave Greece a month earlier: 'You yourself will return to Egypt first opportunity'. On the next day a further message announced the arrival that night of two Sunderlands and provided carefully drawn-up passenger lists with a rendezvous at Sphakia at 8.45 in the evening. Each flying boat was to evacuate 34 people.

The two Sunderlands left Alexandria in the late afternoon, timing their flights to arrive off Sphakia just after dark to avoid German fighters: they were 230 Squadron's L2166 commanded by Flight Lieutenant Brand assisted by Flying Officer Milligan,[250] and 228 Squadron's T9046 under Flight Lieutenant Frame with Sergeant

Massam. The flying boats flew low. As with Icarus of ancient legend, whose flight from the tyrannical King Minos of Crete ended when the wax in the feather wings made for him by his father Daedalus melted in the sun, danger lay in height and sunshine. Up there, in the bright Mediterranean light the yellow-nosed Me 109s ruled. But low down, in the darkness, before Homer's 'fresh and rosy-fingered dawn', at wave-top level, Sunderlands found safety.

228 Squadron's Order No 138 of 30 May recited that 'There is a large number of Military and RAF personnel including the G.O.C. Crete (Freyberg) ... to be evacuated from Sphakia ... The beach is being bombed and machine gunned in the day time and sometimes at night ... Surface wind light variable ... ' The Sunderlands were to leave Alexandria at 1700 hours and proceed to the vicinity of Gaudo Island off Sphakia. Brand was to land first, 'as late as possible consistent with sufficient light for landing, and proceed to dinghies'. Frame was to follow after a short interval. Engines were to be switched off as soon as feasible after landing to minimise detection from exhaust flames. The aircraft were to load as quickly as possible and return independently to Aboukir Bay. A vertical searchlight, like the Alexandrian 'Pharos' of ancient times, would be lit from 1.30 am to guide the flying boats in.[251]

Figure 52: General Freyberg (centre) in a cave at Sphakia, waiting for evacuation by Sunderland, 29 May 1941. The general's personal assistant throughout the period, John White, identified the activity as the pouring of the general's customary evening gin, lime, and water by his batman, Private Hall. Sharing it with him is Captain J.A.V. Morse, Chief Naval Officer, Crete. *Collection of J.C. White.*

As is almost inevitable in the 'fog of war', events did not unfold quite so simply. Brand's L2166 found its party of evacuees, which included General Freyberg and his personal staff.[252] Frame's T9046, however, had difficulty locating its passengers:

> ... two members of the crew rowed ashore in a dinghy, but found no trace of anyone. On returning to the aircraft they spotted a light flickering on Gaudhos island and realised that their position was six miles to the south-west of their destination. Frame at once taxied to the correct position where a boat with the passengers aboard was located.[253]

T9046's difficulties are represented in Alec's logbook in the cryptic comments '2¼ hours on water – taxied six miles'. The hitch cannot have been pleasant for either the Sunderlanders or the waiting evacuees. Twenty-six passengers were embarked, including Freyberg's Chief of Staff, Brigadier Stewart,[254] and Brigadier G.S. Brunskill, known as 'Bruno' and described by Lieutenant Elliott as 'the presiding administrative genius in Crete . . . with a face like an axe and a black patch over the left eye which had been blown out in the last war'.[255] The journey back to Egypt took three and a half hours.[256]

Dan Davin recounts the evacuation from the Creforce point of view, reporting that Freyberg, Beamish, Stewart, and other key personnel gathered at 8.45 pm in the RAF cave, in which the last operational radio was located, and, when the Sunderlands arrived, passed through Brigadier Inglis's cordon controlling access to the shore. Freyberg ordered Inglis to join the departing party and his protests were 'sharply overruled'. Davin quotes Freyberg:

> My own feelings can be imagined better than described. I was handing over a difficult situation with the enemy through in one place almost to the beaches from which we were to make our last attempt to get away the remnants of the fighting force that still held out, tired, hungry, and thirsty on the heights above.[257]

The exhausted evacuees, and their Sunderland crews, arrived back at Aboukir Bay at midnight and 2 am respectively: 'hot food and beds were available for the whole party in the Officers' Mess'.[258] The New Zealand Prime Minister, apparently recovered from his car crash four days earlier, was on hand to greet them as they came ashore from the Sunderlands. Fraser later told James Thorn: 'At midnight, accompanied by Mr Berendsen, I went by motor car to Aboukir airport to meet General Freyberg, Brigadier Stewart and others who had returned to Egypt in accordance with orders from General Wavell.'[259] German radio reported that Freyberg's aircraft had been shot down, a propaganda ploy which could be exposed once the general was visibly in Egypt.[260]

Figure 53: A group of 228 and 230 Squadron Sunderland pilots, Alexandria, 1941. The caption to this picture (CM 747) in the Imperial War Museum reads: 'A group of Royal Air Force flying boat pilots, who did such magnificent work in connection with the British withdrawal from Greece'. This suggests it was taken in May 1941 – before the evacuation of Crete, which would otherwise surely have been mentioned. Quite a few identifications are possible, some with less certainty than others. Alec is seated in the centre of the middle row with hands on knee, fifth from the left. Dundas Bednall identifies the 230 Squadron pilots Lionel Powell (far left), Odhams (third from left), 'Scruffy' Woodward (seated front), Flight Lieutenant (later Wing Commander and DFC) A.M.G. Lywood, subsequently Commanding Officer of 228 Squadron from 1944 to its disbandment in 1945, and the writer of the foreword to John Evans's history of the squadron (centre back), and Flight Lieutenant Brand, whose Sunderland accompanied Alec's to Crete a few weeks later (second from right). At our meeting, Bill Goldfinch pointed out J.C. Paré, who flew with Alec on several missions (second from left). Pilot Officer L.G.M. Rees, who 'borrowed' T9046 during Alec's leave after Crete to carry out an open-sea rescue on 8 June 1941, seems identifiable (fourth from left) from the Kampala picture on page 165[Fig.55]. *Imperial War Museum CM747.*

But was the real political triumph not Fraser's presence in a far-off war zone to urge further efforts to evacuate forces from Crete and to greet his battle-weary rearguard warriors in their escape and distress? A few days later, the New Zealand Prime Minister addressed the tired but now safe troops:

> You were literally blasted out of Crete by an air attack no flesh and blood could stand. You have proved beyond doubt that parachute troops can be defeated. By doing that you have achieved a great victory not only for your own country but also for the Motherland. After what you did in Crete it is unlikely that any German parachutists will ever land in the United Kingdom.[261]

Peter Fraser's attributes as a thinker and statesman would slowly come to be appreciated in London following his arrival there on 21 June 1941. Churchill's secretary, John Colville, initially reported that 'Mr Fraser, the dull Prime Minister of New Zealand, came to lunch' with Churchill at Chequers, but a biographical footnote, composed subsequently, conceded that 'Once his shyness was penetrated, gold shone and he was seen to be a sincere, unassuming and deep-thinking statesman.'[262]

On 31 May, the next night, T9046 made a further and last journey back to Sphakia; the team on the flight deck was Frame, Pilot Officer Paré, and Sergeant Massam. Alec's own report tells the story of this final sortie to Crete:

> On arrival at the coast of Crete we flew along a six mile stretch of the coast searching for Sphakia Bay, and flashing the prearranged letter at likely looking spots. No replies were received. At 2125 hours we alighted off Sphakia Bay and started to taxi inshore. We then saw a light flashing S.O.S. ashore and taxied towards it. The other Sunderland alighted abreast of us about this time. On proceeding ashore by rubber dinghy my second pilot discovered a party of about 20 Greek soldiers and an RAF Flight Lieutenant, who informed him that the party we were supposed to collect were 2 miles further along the coast. We took aboard six of the most important looking Greeks including two walking wounded. One soldier swam out to the aircraft so we took him also . . . We followed up the coast and taxied into Sphakia Manch. Apart from the other aircraft no notice was taken of our light

signals to the shore. The other Sunderland told me that they were unable to find any more people interested in a flight to Egypt and that they were returning. This was about 0030 hours 1/6/41. After they had taken off I taxied close inshore and endeavoured by flashing to get someone interested in us. Everyone, however, seemed fully occupied loading onto H.M. ships. The only reply received to a query as to the whereabouts of our party was 'Do not know' . . . At 0108 hours I took off for the return flight.[263]

The RAF officer rescued was Flight Lieutenant D.S.G. Honor, a Hurricane pilot from 274 Squadron shot down on 25 May after destroying two German aircraft over Maleme. He survived on the run for six days with the assistance of Cretan peasants and a party of Greek soldiers. Honor later told *The Times*:

Night came on and we saw the Me 109's ground strafing a nearby aerodrome. When we heard an aircraft approaching the island we thought it was German until I saw the shape of a Sunderland. We started signalling with pocket torches and I sent out messages in Morse. My 'RAF here – RAF here', in torchlight saved me, although in the Sunderland pilot's words it was a million to one chance. The Sunderland's crew had to inflate their dinghy in order to take us on board.[264]

The confusion and surrealism on shore at Sphakia as the distressing decisions about priority for evacuation were made and enforced is well evoked in Dan Davin's account. As one of those responsible, Brigadier Hargest told Davin:

I was exhausted and the continual importuning was terribly hard to resist – I felt it would be easier to stay . . . Later in the moonlight three small ships appeared, the MLC's. They came slowly up to the beach and put their prows down. We sat on in perfect peace. Then a dark shape appeared low in the sky. A Hun – no – a Sunderland Flying Boat. It dipped and landed somewhere out of sight.[265]

Alec's logbook entry for the final return from Crete betrays sheer exhaustion from the relentless sorties, the depressing effect of continuing chaos and retreat, and frustration at the impossibility of saving more from harm or imprisonment. The four exclamation marks in what follows are unique in all the logbooks. The entry not only overlooks the rescue of the gallant Hurricane pilot, but is also uncharacteristically unfair to the Greek allies:

> Crete – Aboukir with 7 Greeks!
> 3 1/2 hrs. on water – effort wasted!!!

This was the last flight out of Crete, and perhaps it typifies the unfortunate course of the short campaign to defend the island. The commander of T9046 no longer knew who was aboard his aircraft, and must also have been unaware of the valiant role of the 8th Greek Infantry Regiment in providing a measure of protection to the withdrawing British and Commonwealth troops, in the course of which it lost more than 60 officers and men.[266]

Two weeks later, on 16 June 1941, 228 Squadron ORB records that 'On the recommendation of the AOC in C . . . His Majesty . . . graciously pleased to award the DFC to Fl. Lt. Alexander Frame . . . for courage, determination and devotion to duty'. The logbook records the date of the award of the Distinguished Flying Cross as 14 July 1941. The official citation of the award was, however, gazetted on 11 July and specified that

> This officer has completed a large number of operational missions since the war began. On one occasion, operating from this country, he carried out a patrol in search of five enemy ships which entailed a flight lasting for thirteen and a half hours. Since December 1940, he has performed excellent work in the Mediterranean zone of operations. During the evacuation from Greece, Flight Lieutenant Frame operated with great success and was responsible for the safe evacuation of over 200 personnel by air. Throughout he has displayed great skill, courage and devotion to duty.[267]

After the return from Crete on 1 June, there is a gap in the logbook until 12 June. Alec, in Alexandria, exhausted and mourning the recent loss of comrades, might have understood the state of mind of Amr, the Arab general who took the city in the year 641 to found an Arab millennium, and is reputed to have said on his deathbed there: 'I feel as if the heaven lay close upon the earth and I between the two, breathing through the eye of a needle.'[268]

A reasonable guess would be that Alec was sent on much-needed leave, perhaps to Palestine or Lebanon, favoured destinations for tired warriors at the time. But in his absence T9046 continued to deliver 'Help from the Heavens', as John Evans has titled his helpful history of 228 Squadron (in translation of the squadron's motto, *'auxilium a caelo'*). On 8 June 1941, with Pilot Officer L.G.M. Rees in command in Alec's absence, T9046 took off from Aboukir Bay in search of two Wellington bombers reported as having force-landed in the sea. A rubber dinghy was spotted with six survivors and, judging them to be in danger of being dashed onto a dangerous coast, Lees decided to land:

> The wind was light but there was a moderate swell running so I made my approach and pancaked on to the swell alongside the rubber dinghy. The inboard motors were switched off and we taxied to get the dinghy alongside . . . The survivors appeared to be in an exhausted condition although cheerful, and I learned from them that they had been in the water for 31 hours . . . I then took off, going across wind and along the swell which was running from 6-8 feet . . . [269]

This has not been a study of generals leading their troops to victory. On the contrary, the centrepiece of this account is not one, but two, successive retreats. Sir Francis Bacon has wisely noted that 'prosperity doth best discover vice, but adversity doth best discover virtue'.[270] Under what circumstances can retreating forces 'keep their shape', if I may use a modern sporting metaphor, sufficiently to preserve themselves for the fight-back and eventual success?

The fall of Crete was said by Paul Freyberg to be 'the lowest point in British fortunes in the Second World War'. It came hard on the heels of the reverse in Greece, with the turning-points of Hitler's invasion of Russia and America's entry into the war still in the future. The 26th of May 1941 is perhaps Churchill's darkest day of the war. On that date it becomes clear that Crete cannot be held against the German airborne attacks. It is uncertain whether evacuation of any part of the forces will be possible. On the same day, the German battleship *Bismarck*, having sunk the *Hood* with heavy loss of life, escapes its pursuers into the Atlantic. A Cabinet meeting in London is tense, the Prime Minister's mood black. But on the next day the mood is reversed: the *Bismarck* is famously sunk and Roosevelt makes his speech asserting the 'freedom of the seas' and promising American patrols to ensure the delivery of supplies to Britain. Churchill recovers his equilibrium.

Towards the end of the war, when General Freyberg said his

farewell to a large part of the New Zealand Division, his 'Special Order of the Day' congratulated his men on the great victories in the Western Desert from Alamein onwards. But it also reminded them that

> I venture to think that we shall look back with the greatest pride to the times when we fought without adequate equipment. It was then that our Star shone brightest, then that our best work was done, holding the enemy in the Middle East until the Allies were organised on a war footing. Greece, Crete, Sidi Rezegh, Minqar Qa'im, and Ruweisat Ridge are names which will be amongst our proudest memories . . . Goodbye, God Speed, Kia Ora Katoa.[271]

The loss of Crete led to some cooling of the long-standing relations between Churchill and Freyberg. The Prime Minister's natural disappointment had been fuelled by Inglis's comments in London that were critical of the conduct of the defence of the island. Not until August the following year, when Churchill visited the victorious New Zealand Division in the Western Desert, was the old warmth re-established. John White reported:

Figure 54. Prime Minister Winston Churchill congratulates General Freyberg (left) and his New Zealand Division in the North African desert, 1942. *Collection of J.C. White*

Mr Churchill drove up in an open car complete with sun helmet, green glasses, siren suit and silk parasol – he looked like a butterfly hunter ... he went round everyone after being met by [Freyberg] and shook hands ... he said 'Call them round, I want to say something to them'. So round everyone gathered, the NZers in a semicircle in front of the Prime Minister ... We shall not forget that he said of the NZ Division: 'You have played a magnificent, a notable and even a decisive part in stemming a great retreat which might have been most detrimental to the whole cause of the British Empire and the United Nations.'[272]

10. Farewell to T9046

The exasperation evident in the logbook entry for the final flight from Sphakia on 1 June 1941, when T9046 flew back half empty, having been unable to find a way through the demoralisation and confusion of the evacuation, is understandable. 228 and 230 Squadron crews were depleted and exhausted from the stresses of the operations for Crete, hard on the heels of those for Greece. Also, in the first week of June Alexandria harbour suffered intensive bombing attacks at night, with hundreds of deaths. Morale must have been strained, with the losses of comrades – in Alec's case, of Henry Lamond and his crew dead or 'in the bag' – and with the repeated scenario of defeat, confusion, and retreat. Of 228 Squadron's complement of Sunderlands, only two remained serviceable: T9046 and L5803.

In June 1941 these weary remnants were ordered to West Africa to join the battle for the Atlantic and the critical fight against the German U-boats. As preparations for departure were made, Churchill replaced General Wavell, who left the Middle East command for the Far East. Freya Stark, an Arabic expert attached to the British Embassy, witnessed the leave-taking in Cairo:

> On the morning of July the 8th, 1941, I drove with Sophie Shone to say good-bye to General Wavell. He was being sent away from us, as C-in-C, to India . . . He looked tired, and sad, and kind, and the huge and empty aerodrome, the sandy edges of the hills, the pale colour-wash – ochre and blue – of the early day, seemed all to lie attendant as a frame to a picture, round the group of uniforms and the weather-beaten faces, and the solitary figure who was handing over the defence of all this world and what it meant . . . The little group, the buff and scarlet and gold, lonely in the bright morning where only the kites were flying, with the camouflaged Lysander lying like some French brig ready to take off into the sea of air, made me think strangely of a Highland farewell in the Stuart wars . . . [273]

Churchill's relations with Wavell had been strained for some time, and on 20 June the Prime Minister had written to the Viceroy of India, Lord Linlithgow, proposing to relieve Wavell as commander in the Middle East and to exchange the positions of Generals Wavell and Auchinleck, the commander in India. Having conceded Wavell's early successes, Churchill wrote: 'I feel he is tired, and that a fresh eye and an unstrained hand is needed.'[274]

The guard was changing. New commanders would be left to direct the progressive strengthening of the British forces as American supply intensified, and their eventual victory in Africa following the battle of El Alamein.

In the early and still-dark hours of 25 June, T9046 rose from Aboukir Bay for the last time, unusually turning south for Khartoum in Sudan. Aboard were Alec, Pilot Officers Brown and Harte-Lovelace and, as navigator, Flying Officer Austin, whose course for the blind take-off at Nauplion had got them through that Greek affair. There were five other crew and five squadron passengers.

Flying Officer John Mason, on board T9046, probably vented the frustration of all ranks when he recorded the vacillations in the squadron's orders in June 1941: 'What an HQ – I give up??' This referred to the succession of orders and counter-orders which had delayed their departure. But when L5083, and then two days later T9046, got off for their journeys across Africa, an incident reported by Mason reminds us of the realities of command of these big, self-sufficient, fighting flying boats. After they had taken off from Aboukir Bay in the pre-dawn of 25 June:

> At 8.30 we received a signal from 201 Group asking us to return to base but Fl/Lt. Frame, the captain of the aircraft, replied and said 'repeat and check signal', at the same time proceeded on the way South to Khartoum. As we did not receive another signal, we carried on, arriving at our moorings at 'Gordon's Tree' at 1.15 pm.[275]

The potential for autonomy in these aircraft was considerable. Unwelcome messages from higher command might not always be received or understood.

The flight took nearly eight hours and on arrival at Khartoum the party was inoculated against yellow fever by the RAF medical officer. During the night a severe *Haboob*[276] uprooted trees and lifted roofs from houses, but the moored Sunderland was undamaged.

The squadron's radio specialist, Carl van der Meulen, was aboard the other Sunderland, L5803, under the unit's new commanding officer, Wing Commander Brooks, and kept a journal of the progress of the two aircraft across Africa. He noted:

> The highlight of the (first) leg, flying, for a change over the uninteresting semi-desert of southern Egypt, was the intercepted news over the radio that Hitler had started to invade Russia ... RAF Khartoum was a memorable experience. No blackout, temperatures 114 degrees F ... Everyone lived in rush huts with beds at least three feet from the 'wall' to frustrate visits from scorpions with a morbid interest in human flesh.[277]

At 3.15 the next morning, T9046 took off from Khartoum for Port Bell, near Kampala, in Uganda. The weather was good and the Sunderland flew at heights from 2000 to 5000 feet. Radio bearings were obtained from several stations en route and these proved accurate and of great assistance in navigating over the trackless wastes. Lake Victoria and Kampala were located after an eight-hour flight, and the squadron ORB noted some unusual preparations for

Figure 55: 228 Squadron officers from Sunderlands T9046 and L5803 on the steps of the Imperial Hotel, Kampala, July 1941. Front row, left to right: Flight Lieutenant Goyen; Flight Lieutenant Frame, DFC; the Commanding Officer, Wing Commander Brooks, DFC; Flight Lieutenant Grunert; Flying Officer Rees. Middle row, left to right: Flying Officer Austin; Flying Officer Mason; Flying Officer Brown; Pilot Officer Harte-Lovelace.

alighting: 'After crocodiles and Hippopotami had been cleared from the landing area a/c became waterborne, and arrived at Port Bell at 1126 GMT'.

There, on 26 June, T9046 met with Brooks's now unserviceable Sunderland L5803. A radio signal asking for a new engine to be carried aboard T9046 had not reached Egypt in time. That was possibly the reason for the disregarded recall mentioned earlier: if so, the commanding officer may not have been pleased. In any case, Alec was sent aloft again to try to send a radio message to Middle East headquarters in Cairo to summon a spare engine. This was not successful, and it was finally decided that the faulty engine should be loaded aboard T9046, which would return to Khartoum for a replacement. The on-the-water transfer operation nearly ended in disaster when the heavy Pegasus engine broke the Sunderland's bomb rack cable.

Figure 56: The only photograph of T9046 known to the author – taken on Lake Victoria, Uganda, July 1941.

During the stay in Kampala, Alec must have received a message that his father had died in Oamaru on 27 June. On 30 June, T9046 left Lake Victoria to retrace the seven-hour flight to Khartoum, returning on 2 July with a new Pegasus engine. Alec looks worn in the picture taken on the steps of the Imperial Hotel in Kampala in July, as well he might given his bereavement, the intensity of recent flying in Greece and Crete, and the successive ferrying flights for the engine for L5803. On his left in the picture is Wing Commander Brooks, DFC, a veteran credited with the first successful Sunderland attack on a submarine in January 1940, and the successor to Nicholetts as the squadron's commander. On his right is Frank Goyen, a popular Australian squadron member, a lover of classical music and a skilful tennis player. In little more than a year, Goyen would command Sunderland W4026 when, on 25 August 1942, with the Duke of Kent as a VIP aboard, the aircraft, off track and in cloud at 700 feet, flew into a hillside at Eagle's Rock in northern Scotland half an hour after take-off from Invergordon. Fourteen men, including the Duke, died in the crash, which has never been definitively explained. Alec was stationed at Alness, near Invergordon, at the time, engaged in training Sunderland crews, and would have felt the loss of this comrade, with whom he had flown and shared dangers and adventures from the earliest days of the war.[278]

On 7 July 1941, with serviceability problems at last under control, T9046 rose from Lake Victoria at dawn, bound westwards for Stanleyville (now Kisangani in Zaire). The squadron ORB recounts that two attempts to take off were unsuccessful, due to the heavy weight of the aircraft and the air-thinning altitude (Lake Victoria is 3700 feet above sea level) and continues:

> . . . aircraft was forced on the first stage through heavy rain and low cloud as far as Lake Albert. An alteration of course was made at Kasenyi to navigate a valley approximately 20 miles wide in a high range of mountains, over which hung large amounts of cumulus cloud.

Stanleyville was reached and a landing made on the River Congo at 11 am. The following day a further flight was made to Leopoldville (now Kinshasa), and on 9 July the Sunderland pushed on to the western coast at Pointe Noire, where, the ORB records: 'Crocodile shoot arranged by the Commandant, Free French Forces. One crocodile was shot, retrieved, and skinned. The skin was 14ft.6. Officers dined with the Commandant in the evening.'

The final leg of the journey was flown on 12 July, when T9046 took off northwards for Lagos in Nigeria. The ORB fixes the position of the flying boat as it crossed the equator, in position 08 20 at 0912 GMT, which the reader may see on the nearby map. At Lagos another feat of mechanical resourcefulness was required when it was discovered that an airscrew blade was split and chipped. With limited equipment, Leading Aircraftsman Bindong balanced the airscrew by making corresponding chips in the other two blades.[279]

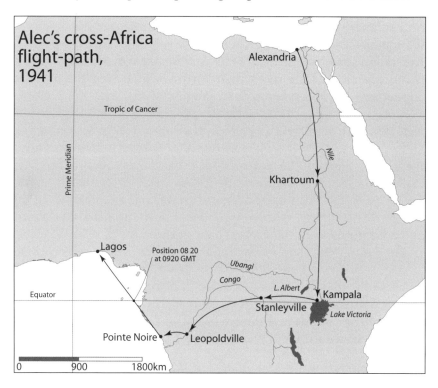

On the same day, 12 July 1941, the New Zealand Prime Minister, Peter Fraser, having continued his journey onwards to London from the Middle East, spoke to a private meeting of the Empire Parliamentary Association held at the House of Commons in Westminster. In the chair was the Right Honourable Clement Attlee – a future prime minister. Fraser delivered this verdict on the recent events in Greece and Crete:

> Take the question of Greece. There was never a question that was more thoroughly discussed and gone into than that of the expedition to Greece. The decisions arrived at were arrived

at after a thorough examination and, as far as New Zealand was concerned, after a more pessimistic appreciation of the position than we got from Britain. So we cannot claim that we were lured into Greece. We cannot claim that we were misled into Greece. We went in there, knowing that it would be exceedingly difficult, but . . . we felt it would be an impossible and disgraceful thing for the British Commonwealth to cheer the Greeks on from the side line when they were facing up to the Italians in Albania, and then run away from them when Hitler came in (hear, hear). We knew that that would mean a complete moral defeat throughout the world and the American Isolationists would rejoice and would have cause for condemning us . . . So far as Crete is concerned, that was more or less an accident, as far as we went, and matters like that will have to be better planned in the future. That is all I am going to say about it.[280]

These remarks have an extemporaneous quality which lends them authority, and we cannot fail to note the relevance of American political perceptions to Fraser's assessment of the reasons for the expedition to Greece.

Sunderland T9046, on my rough count from the logbook, flew nearly 600 hours under my father's command between December 1940 and August 1941, when pilot and machine were joined for the last time on the journey to home waters, leaving West Africa on 24 August, the day on which Prime Minister Churchill broadcast from Chequers to the nation on his first meeting with President Roosevelt in Placentia Bay, Newfoundland. As Jimmy Roosevelt had so controversially observed three months earlier, America was in the war in all but name.

Sunderland T9046 had left Bathurst in West Africa for Gibraltar, and there, on 28 August, boarded two very distinguished passengers: Lord Gort, VC,[281] and Admiral Somerville,[282] for the journey across the Bay of Biscay towards the southern coast of England, where the flying boat alighted at the familiar Mount Batten base. Three days later, the two military commanders were reported by Churchill's private secretary, John Colville, as dining at Chequers to discuss the defence of Gibraltar. The Prime Minister, 'who would not stop talking', prolonged the proceedings until three in the morning.[283] Somerville's account of the purpose of the meeting was blunt: to dispose of 'some of the wet ideas about Gib that were in active circulation and emanating chiefly from Chequers'.[284]

The return to Mount Batten made full-circle for the Sunderland. The departure with Henry Lamond, although a mere nine months earlier, must have seemed a lifetime ago to my father against the density of experience which pilot and machine had seen in the intervening period. T9046 had been the nearest thing to home for Alec, as well as a companion to be nursed through the stress and strain of action.

The final days of T9046 after the return from Africa would be with 95 Squadron, first at Calshot and then, fatally, back to the Mediterranean. The damage it had sustained has been chronicled in these pages: from the storm in Kalafrana Bay in January 1941, bullet holes from Muncheberg's Me 109s at Saint Paul's Bay in March, 'friendly-fire' tail damage over Kalamata in April, and the mechanical wear and tear which manifested itself on the cross-Africa journey in July.

The Sunderland had seen the faces of defeat, and had sheltered exhausted and wounded soldiers and airmen in the evacuations of Greece and Crete. And distinguished passengers too: Wavell, Longmore, General Mackay, Jimmy Roosevelt, General Freyberg's staff from Crete, Lord Gort, and Admiral Somerville among them.

We know the flying boat's subsequent end and resting-place also, from this account of an incident at Kalafrana Bay in Malta on Saturday 21 February 1942:

> During the early hours of the 21st another Sunderland – T9046 of 95 Squadron flown by Flight Lt. W. Bocock – arrived from Gibraltar following an 11 hour flight carrying ten more new fighter pilots . . . The flying boat was to leave again that night . . . and was being prepared for departure when a Bf 109 swept in at low level, guns blazing – damage was caused to the starboard wing and tail section. A second fighter was only prevented from attacking by the intense light AA fire. The damage was deemed repairable, but rough seas caused the boat to keel over, and despite attempts to put her right, part of the starboard wing eventually broke off below water; T9046 subsequently sank during a storm two days later.[285]

So ended the life of T9046: in duration not much more than two years, but in intensity and range of activity, particularly in the Mediterranean spring of 1941, one of quality and note.

Alec's war continued. After West Africa it was back to RAF home waters. Then again to Aboukir Bay for a period with 230 Squadron that was notable for two attacks on submarines. In 1943, after the formation of 490 (New Zealand) Squadron and training in the cold and storms of northern Scotland at Alness, Alec was sent with the squadron to West Africa to join the anti-submarine and convoy protection effort in the Atlantic. A pleasant interlude opened up for three crews who were sent to America on the *Queen Elizabeth* to take delivery of three new Catalina aircraft for ferrying to West Africa. Alec, by now a squadron leader, was one of the lucky three captains, and in his crew was a fellow Oamaruvian and old Waitakian, Flying Officer W.J. Dodds. After a four-day crossing at 30 knots on the famous liner, the crews travelled by rail to Montreal, where the officers were accommodated at the Windsor Hotel, and on to Dorval, the hub of Ferry Command in Canada. The informal 490 Squadron diary takes up the story: 'New York was only 10 hours away and we had a marvellous time. Night clubs, parties, tennis, baseball, sightseeing . . . Eggs, steak, chicken . . . '[286]

'After weeks of waiting', apparently not uncomfortably, Alec and his crew went by train to Elizabeth City in North Carolina, where they took delivery of a new Mark 4 JX Catalina straight off the assembly line. After the necessary checks, the long-range twin-engined flying boat set off on 15 September 1943 via Bermuda, Gander, and Newfoundland for the 12¾-hour flight across the Atlantic to Largs, near Glasgow on the western coast of Scotland. The arrival is marked in the logbook by a rare set of three exclamation marks celebrating this first transatlantic flight: 'At. Cross !!!' Did the weary pilot making landfall and letting down into Largs Bay allow himself to think of his grandmother, Mary Paterson, a child factory-worker who could not write, setting out for Dunedin in New Zealand across these waters in the ship *Mairi Bhan* nearly 70 years before, and of his grandfather, 'Stoker' Alex, aboard the iron ship *Jessie Readman* in the same year?

The transatlantic crew returned to 490 Squadron by ferrying Catalina 1B, registration FP 112, dubbed *Marlborough*, south to Freetown in West Africa, arriving on 20 October 1943, when Alec and his crew rejoined their comrades with some festivity. The party was highly rated in the squadron's informal diary: 'ring leaders were F/Lt. Outram and F/O Shephard who were unrestrainable'.[287]

Within a few days, however, Alec was transferred to the nearby 204 Squadron at Bathurst as its new flight commander. On 18

November 1943, Catalina *Marlborough*, now under the command of Flight Lieutenant R.M. Grant, crashed at Iron Ore Creek near Freetown, with loss of all but one of the seven crew members, including Alec's close friend Bill Dodds.[288] The pilot of the aircraft appears to have misjudged his height above that old flying-boat enemy, a 'flat calm' water surface.

Although under-recorded in the histories, the Sunderland, with its flight and ground crews, played a significant and noteworthy role in that phase of the Mediterranean war in 1941 which saw the evacuations from Greece and, soon after, from Crete. Historical accounts are inclined to describe the contribution of the flying-boat squadrons as 'neglected' or 'unsung', although I never heard my father speak in this way. If there has been neglect, the reasons are not difficult to understand.

The first has to do with the military context of their exploits. Although military reverses can produce feats of arms by the losing side which are admired – the Spartan sacrifice at Thermopylae is an example – it must be remembered that the sequence of British evacuations in the war against Hitler had become embarrassingly long: Norway, Dunkirk, Greece, and Crete. As Churchill famously told the House of Commons in June 1940 in relation to the Dunkirk evacuation: 'We must be very careful not to assign to this deliverance the attributes of victory . . . Wars are not won by evacuations.'[289]

The evacuations from Greece and Crete were looking repetitious, less providential, and progressively less orderly than earlier withdrawals. Even Churchill had run out of mitigating explanations. In mid-1941, neither the leaders nor the peoples of Britain, Australia, and New Zealand much desired to dwell on the events of, or the reasons for, the continuing military calamities in the Mediterranean. The flying boats and their crews were a part, however creditable, of a 'bad news' story. Soon, better news would come with the resupply and renewal of the British forces in Africa, and as progress was made towards the defeat of Rommel at El Alamein and the driving of the Afrika Korps from the theatre. In June 1941, the German invasion of Russia provided a new story with new names and places. These were events which could provide uplifting war reporting for the home front.

A second reason has to do with perceptions of the role of the RAF in the two campaigns of Greece and Crete, and of its apparent inability to provide fighter protection and ground support to the troops. In both campaigns, a significant, and perhaps the principal, military cause of the British withdrawals was this German mastery in the air. Inevitably, it led to the question: 'Where was the RAF?' An eye-witness to the evacuation of Crete at Sphakia, J.K. Elliott, reported:

> I saw troops boo the remnants of the RAF at the evacuation but one could hardly look for logic in the remnant of a force that had been exposed for two weeks to an air attack unprecedented in history for its duration, intensity and ferocity.[290]

The question was natural from soldiers on the ground enduring dive-bombing from Stukas, or strafing from Me 109s, but it would also come from higher echelons of command. Churchill himself became involved, sending this prickly message to Air Chief Marshal Longmore on 29 March 1941:

> I have been concerned to read your continual complaints of the numbers of aircraft which are sent you ... Every conceivable effort has been made under my express directions to reinforce you by every route and method for the last five months ... We are as fully informed as you on what you are getting ... I fear there must be some talk emanating from your Headquarters which is neither accurate nor helpful ... [291]

There had been an earlier occasion for prime ministerial displeasure with his former aviation mentor. In February 1941 Churchill's eagle eye had noticed a message from Longmore to the Air Ministry detailing complaints about the supply of aircraft in which Anthony Eden and General Dill were referred to as 'Anthony' and 'John' respectively. In the cutting manner which must have caused distress to many British commanders during the war, the Prime Minister wrote to the Chief of the Air Staff, Air Marshal Portal:

> I do not like the tone of this telegram. ACM Longmore has shown himself very unappreciative of the immense efforts we are making to support him ... At every stage throughout this Libyan affair we have had to press him forward beyond his judgment or inclination ... It is not customary to speak of the Foreign Secretary and CIGS by their Christian names in this way, and a hint to this effect might well be given.[292]

The deterioration of relations between Churchill and Longmore was to end in the latter's replacement. Abruptly recalled to London on 30 April 1941, ostensibly for consultations, he was not permitted to return to the Middle East. The RAF leaders struggled to persuade Churchill and the other service leaders that serviceable aircraft were only one of two requirements for effective intervention – the other was airfields. These were lost to the RAF in both Greece and Crete. Churchill also had difficulty understanding the effect of climate on the serviceability of aircraft in the Middle East, constantly overestimating Longmore's resources in operational aircraft.

Longmore described his journey home along the now traditional route, Alexandria–Malta–Gibraltar–Mount Batten:

> . . . unescorted flying boats had to time their arrival at Malta so that the last hour in the air was done at night in order to avoid interception by German fighters. My Sunderland approached the island about 11 pm and found a big raid in progress which prevented the flare-path floats in Calafrana Bay being lit. We watched the fire-works for about an hour before permission was given for us to land.[293]

Longmore arrived in London on 5 May 1941 and found it to be 'very war-torn and drab . . . Everyone seemed much thinner, a little weary, slightly on edge, but the spirit to endure was very evident.' Soon he was attending late-night Defence Committee meetings deep below ground.,'The Prime Minister was in the chair, wearing his syren suit and smoking his cigar. He seemed to be in excellent form, very much in charge of proceedings and apparently relishing his vast responsibilities in framing future war plans.'

But Longmore was quickly made to realise that there would be no return to his Middle East command: 'My personal feelings are better left to the imagination. It seemed that this change had already been planned when the signal recalling me to England for consultations had been sent.'[294] Longmore, who had loyally carried out his orders, and had borne the responsibility of sending men to their deaths in near-hopeless air actions, was summarily discarded and sent home to his wife in Grantham, to potter about with ambulances. Although his RAF career was later resumed, the episode must be counted one of the least charitable actions of the British wartime leadership.

His successor, Air Marshal Tedder, wrote in June 1941:

There is, as I expected, a first-class hate working up in the
Army against the Royal Air Force for having 'let them down'
in Greece and Crete. Wavell is very worried about it and is
doing his best to stamp on it. But I am not sure that even now
the real reasons for the lack of air support are appreciated in
higher places in the Army here.[295]

For the flying-boat squadrons themselves, new tasks and new
technologies loomed. The Battle of the Atlantic was entering a critical
phase in which Sunderlands and Catalinas would play an important
part in convoy protection and submarine-attack roles from home
waters and from West Africa. Radar, Leigh lights, depth-charges,
improved Sunderlands with more reliable engines – these would be
the new concerns for the flying-boat units.

But the Mediterranean period in 1941, when two Sunderland
squadrons, with a handful of serviceable aircraft, operating mainly
from makeshift bases in an environment in which the enemy had
general numerical ascendancy in the air, remains a notable episode
in the history of flying boats in war. The Sunderlands and their
pilots, crew, and ground-support staff, were a vital support for the
British command structure by moving key political and military
leaders and vital technical personnel in and out of precarious battle
zones. For the pilots, there would be no period of the war in which
their services were more relied upon, their skills, endurance, and
self-reliance more tested, or their *esprit de corps* more essential.

Afterwards, for my father there was more war in flying boats,
but a new family also. Alec met my mother, 'Penny', formerly Grace
Davidson, the youngest daughter of a Scots medical doctor, in 1942.
She had overstated her age to join the WAAF. She told us of a walk
up to Arthur's Seat in Edinburgh early in their courtship, and they
were married at Holy Trinity Church in Tulse Hill, London, on 4
June 1943.

And children. Our initials and dates of birth appear in the
logbook, illegally but significantly. And travel. To Sydney in 1951 to
fly the Sunderland-derived Solents and Hythes to Hobart and Lord
Howe Island with the short-lived Trans Oceanic Airways, and on
to Tahiti in 1953 for that decade of blue lagoons and 'other drums'
with which this story began.

Alec was a careful man, meticulous without being fussy,
especially where the sea and elements were concerned. We children
water-skied under his care in Tahitian lagoons, and later in my

teenage years in New Zealand I fished with him quite a bit from a small open boat with an outboard motor. The rods and reels, and the tackle box with its compartments of hooks, swivels, weights, and lures, were always well ordered. Corrosion was an old enemy, and gear was washed in fresh water after use, oiled, checked. The motor was worked conservatively, even nursed. I was 'crew' and the orders were always quiet but firm, and there was often a chuckle shared about some unexpected difficulty. The habit of command had become so practised with Alec that it was almost unnoticeable by the commanded.

That was how he flew as well, and no doubt one of the reasons why, in all those entries in the logbooks over 30 years and 7500 hours of flight, the most serious of the very rare pilot-controllable mishaps, in war or in peace, is the damaged float when attempting an open-sea landing to pick up survivors from the *Empire Merchant* in the North Sea in August 1940 – and that must be reckoned a risk justified by the circumstances. Of course, Alec and his comrades are unlikely to have thought in this way; they were closer to the professional gambler: you died when your 'number was up', no sense in worrying about what could not be helped.

Here is a curious paradox. Not much interested in history, perhaps even dismissive of it, my father was yet the faithful keeper of these logbooks which have made possible the reconstructions attempted here. I remember being quite shocked by his casual throwing out of bits of family history as we moved houses in my childhood. As with many of his generation, looking back meant revisiting the humiliations of the Depression and the wrenching emotions of war. But I think there was an ingrained professional reason for my father's attention to the now and the next. Those are the quarters from which danger is coming – that unexpected storm, enemy fighter, engine failure, or coral head. Something can usually be done to avoid or parry the effects of these if anticipated or detected in time, and it is by close attention to such immediate matters that pilots may best hope to protect their passengers, crew, and themselves. From that perspective, history is at best an idle diversion and at worst a dangerous distraction.

In April 2005 the waters of Marsaxlokk Bay in Malta lapped at the *luzzu*, fishing boats bright-painted in greens, yellows, and blues. The old Kalafrana base at the mouth of the bay is now obliterated by the huge cranes and container stacks of the 'Freeport Terminal'. But the wartime flying-boat slipway and Sunderland hangar in

Marsaxlokk village further up the bay are still there, serving fishing boats and fish-farming now. Towering across the bay is the smokestack of the Delimara power station with its winking lights warning the jets bringing tourists into nearby Luqa airport. Just off the jetty at the foot of the smokestack are the old flying-boat moorings where Sunderland T9046 sank in a storm in February 1942 after being strafed and set on fire by a Messerschmitt fighter. I learned that the wreck had been removed some years earlier. Now there will be only some fragments of duralumin on the seabed 20 feet down, and perhaps a few spoons from the galley.

My father here 64 years ago was surrounded by the camaraderie and song of crew and officers' mess and the collective routines of squadron life. I am solitary, wandering the bay and the slipway, circling the target, looking for a way into the past. Yesterday, in Saint John's Cathedral in Malta's capital, Valletta, I admired Caravaggio's 1607 painting of *St. Jerome Writing*. The subject is alone, pen in hand, with only a gaping human skull on his table for company, the scene lit by Caravaggio's trademark flash of light. The image catches the predicament of the time-travelling writer, the flux of life towards death, and the link between our forefathers and ourselves, the flight we share across the chasm of time.

In the late afternoon of 21 June 1983, in a slight south-easterly swell with overcast conditions and light showers, the barometer reading 1010, the motor-tugboat *Canterbury* positioned itself at the mouth of Lyttelton Harbour near Christchurch. The master, Captain F. Dawson, ordered the engines to be placed on 'standby', the ensign dipped, and the crew mustered on the quarterdeck. The skipper spoke these words as the ashes of 'Flying Boat Alex', as I think we must now call him, were dispersed in the sea:

> For as much as it hath pleased Almighty God to take unto himself the soul of our dead comrade A. Frame here departed, we commit his last mortal remains to the Four Winds and the Seven Seas in sure and certain hope of the Resurrection to eternal life through our Lord Jesus Christ.

The 'Four Winds and the Seven Seas' were certainly familiar to my father, criss-crossed and caressed in flight, and I think of him as returning home to Te Moana Nui a Kiwa – the Pacific Ocean – not far north of the Oamaru of his birth and childhood.

Notes

1   Arthur Williams, 'W.G. Sebald (1944–2001)',*The Literary Encyclopedia*, www.litencyc.com

2   Homer, *The Odyssey*, translated by Edward McCrorie, with introduction by Richard P. Martin, Johns Hopkins University Press, Baltimore, 2004, Book 8, line 572 (p.117).

3   This aircraft was a Sandringham VII, Bermuda Class, one of only three built to provide a luxury service on the Baltimore–Bermuda run. Essentially a civil version of the wartime Sunderland, it joined the BOAC fleet in 1948 under the name *St George*, was purchased by P.G. (later Sir Gordon) Taylor for £20,000, and flown to Australia in 1954, serving as a specialty tourism transport in the Pacific islands until its acquisition by RAI in 1958 to ferry passengers between Tahiti and the aerodrome in Bora Bora. My father did 1314 hours in this aircraft, mostly on short flights – so a great number of take-offs and landings. It sat abandoned for many years at Fa'aa airport in Tahiti, where it was recovered by the son of Captain Douglas Pearson (another World War II Sunderland hand in West Africa, who subsequently joined Alec at RAI in Tahiti in 1958) and given to the French air museum at Le Bourget, where it is now on display in its old RAI colours.

4   This aircraft had been acquired when Alec was sent by RAI to America in 1956 to select a Catalina from 'mothballed' stock. The Consolidated PBY-5A model had been retired from US Navy use in 1950. It was ferried to Tahiti in March 1957 by Alec with the veteran American aviator Clyde Pangborn.

5   Antoine de Saint-Exupéry, *Terre des Hommes*, Heinemann, London, 1951, p.33. Translation by the present author. Part of the mystery of Saint-Ex's disappearance in 1944 has recently been solved with the discovery, reported in April 2004, of the wreck of his Lockheed Lightning on the ocean floor less than two miles off the French Mediterranean coast between Marseilles and Cassis.

6   Maurice McGreal, *A Noble Chance: One Pilot's Life*, McGreal, Wellington, 1994. Both Alec and Mauri married WAAF girls and brought them back to the South Pacific after the war.

7   Quoted in Curtis Cate, *Antoine de Saint-Exupéry: His Life and Times*, Heinemann, London, 1970, p.322.

8   Grumman built 59 of these elegant twin-engined tricycle-undercarriaged amphibians between 1946 and 1951. The Air Tahiti Mallard F-OAII was J29 (the 29th to be built, in 1947) and was first owned by the Ford Motor Company of Detroit. Alec last flew it on a 'mercy flight' between Huahine and Papeete in November 1955 before it was sold to William C. Wold & Associates of New York City. The Air Pacific Mallard F-BC was J13, which had previously served as Lord Beaverbrook's personal aircraft, and then in the 1960s as a link to the Manapouri power scheme at Deep Cove in the South Island of New Zealand. See Fred W. Hoston and Matthew E. Rodina

Jr, *Grumman Mallard: The Enduring Classic*, Robin Brass Studio Inc, Montreal, 2006, pp.168 and 170.

9   Keith Ovenden, *A Fighting Withdrawal*, Oxford University Press, Oxford, 1996, p.173.

10   Janet Frame, *To the Is-land*, The Women's Press, Auckland, 1983, p.12.

11   Frame, p.12.

12   IM 15/137, Archives New Zealand, Wellington. The *Mairi Bhan* carried some 440 assisted passengers, 352 Scots, and 88 Irish, among them 35 'general servants'.

13   Frame, p.13.

14   Frame, p.53.

15   Frame, p.67.

16   Frame, p.68.

17   May Williamson to Michael King, 26 February 1996. I had put the late Michael King in touch with Auntie May when he was researching his well-known and valuable biography of Janet Frame, and he was kind enough to send me a copy of the resulting letter. Uncle Tom (1911–72), an old Waitakian, served in North Africa as a sergeant in the 7th New Zealand Anti-Tank Regiment, in the thick of Rommel's tank attack at Sidi Rezegh in November 1941. See E.H. Smith, 'Guns Against Tanks', *New Zealand in the Second World War*, Dept of Internal Affairs, Wellington, 1948.

18   *Oamaru Mail*, 30 June, 1941. H. Pheloung (1852?–1909) was an early North Otago figure famed for his work with brass band music. He came to Port Chalmers on the *Jessie Readman* in 1874.

19   See Gavin McLean, *Oamaru Harbour: Port in a Storm*, Dunmore Press, Palmerston North, 1982, p.82.

20   James Bertram, Introduction to Ian Milner, *Milner of Waitaki*, John McIndoe, Dunedin, 1983, p.12.

21   Milner, p.93.

22   My aunt, and Alec's sister, May Williamson, wrote to Janet Frame on 21 October 1963 to welcome her cousin back to New Zealand. She wrote: '37 Wharfe St. Oamaru has been sold and is to be pulled down. I dare not think of it. To me it has always been Home.' Papers of May Williamson.

23   This Milner was the Rector's son Hugh. For an engaging evocation of emotional and intellectual life at Waitaki Boys' High at the time, and the talents and tragedies of members of the Rector's family, including Hugh Milner, see James McNeish, *Dance of the Peacocks*, Random House New Zealand, 2003.

24   Frank Milner, 'Diary of Trip', Ms Papers 0051–064, Alexander Turnbull Library, Wellington.

25   Sir Arthur Longmore, *From Sea to Sky*, Geoffrey Bles, London, 1946, p.135. Longmore added: 'To those who ask what is the use of these races . . . I would reply that we owed the Spitfire to the Schneider Trophy Races. It forced the designer of the air-frame to try new methods and take big technical risks which he would never otherwise have taken.'

26   John Mulgan, *Report on Experience*, Blackwood & Janet Paul, Auckland, 1967, p.10.

27   *Municipal History of Oamaru*, Oamaru Borough Council, 1936, p.83. The population of Oamaru was by then 7486.

28   'Methods of Entry into the RAF by New Zealanders 1919–1938', AIR 118/56, Archives New Zealand, Wellington. 'The first batch of candidates

under the scheme arrived in England in July 1937, and thereafter parties of from twelve to twenty sailed at approximately monthly intervals for the next two years. The total number sent was 241.'

29   The application form and referee report were obtained from New Zealand Defence Force Personnel Archives, Trentham Military Camp, Wellington. James McDiarmid (1871–1943), a prominent businessman with a shoemaking business in Thames Street, had been Mayor of Oamaru between 1919 and 1927. In 1895 he had married Agnes, daughter of Robert Bain, and was probably related to Jemima Frame.

30   Lists of the selected applicants, and notes on their subsequent histories, are in AIR 118/76 (a)–(f), Archives New Zealand, Wellington.

31   For an excellent account of *Centaurus*'s journey, see Phillip E. Sims, *Adventurous Empires*, AirLife Publishing, Shrewsbury, 2000, pp.169–72. John Weir Burgess was born in Dunedin in 1908 and attended Wellington College in the 1920s. His flying career took him to the RAF (1931–35), Imperial Airways, Tasman Empire Airways (TEAL), and BOAC. He died in Sydney in 1993 at the age of 85. 'In the two million miles he flew between 1930 and 1950 he never had a crash, hardly even a mishap', commented Guyon Espiner in 'Flying the Empire', *Evening Post*, 24 September 1994. The Pan American Sikorsky, commanded by Captain Ed Musick, was lost with all aboard on 11 January 1938 out of Pago Pago in Samoa, apparently in an explosion while dumping fuel to lighten the aircraft for return to Pago Pago to attend to a relatively minor mechanical problem. The first recipient in 1938 of the Musick Memorial Trophy, created by public subscription in Auckland in memory of Captain Musick, was Arthur Gouge.

32   AIR 118/76(b), Archives New Zealand, Wellington.

33   The similarity begins with their respective RAF service numbers: Charles Ewen Wilders Evison was 40614, Alexander Frame 40615. Both men trained at No 3 Flying Training School at South Cerney in 1938, being subsequently selected for flying-boat training at Calshot. They joined the first Sunderland-equipped RAF Squadron (210) at Pembroke Dock together on 19 June 1939, and later in the war were successively to command 204 Squadron in West Africa. 'Shorty' Evison was born in Invercargill on 27 March 1916, educated at Ashburton High School, joined the RAF in January 1938, and commanded 204 Squadron, West Africa, in 1943. He was seconded to BOAC in 1944–45. Evison returned to New Zealand and became Flying Control Officer at Mechanics Bay in Auckland in 1946 and later at Laucala Bay in Fiji. John Cooper of Auckland, serving with the Sunderland-equipped 5 Squadron RNZAF, remembers him in Fiji in the mid-1950s, and later living in Remuera Road in Auckland in the 1980s. The *New Zealand Herald* of 22 October 1992 records the making of a special award to Charles Evison for long service as a pedestrian-crossing supervisor at nearby Meadowbank School. Shorty is reported as saying of the schoolchildren he protected, 'They're proper hooligans some of them, but I like them. They're funny a lot of the time.'

34   Many of these details were found in Errol W. Martyn's helpful publication, *For Your Tomorrow*, Volplane Press, Christchurch, 1998. The two volumes record the dates and circumstances of the deaths of New Zealand airmen in war.

35   Dundas Bednall, *Sun on My Wings*, Paterchurch Publications, Pembroke Dock, 1989, p.24. Bednall trained at Abu Sueir, an RAF station in the Middle

East. He was later with 230 Squadron on Sunderlands in Alexandria, and had a distinguished record with that unit.

36 Details on these flying boats may be found in G.R. Duval's helpful *British Flying-Boats and Amphibians 1909–1952*, Putnam, London, 1966

37 'A Guy from Coastal Command: the Autobiography of Group Captain G.A. Bolland, CBE', typescript with photographs, X003-1877, RAF Museum Library, Hendon, London.

38 *The Times*, 23 June 1939. The story was headed 'Misty Weather for RAF Escort' and reported that 'Three Stranraer aircraft from Calshot, which had previously met the ship, retired when the main escort aircraft arrived'. Either the 210 Squadron Sunderlands were overlooked or mistaken for the Stranraers. Another possibility is that the Sunderlands were the 'real' escort, and operated under military secrecy.

39 Saint-Exupéry, p.36. Translation by the present author.

40 L. Baveystock, *Wavetops at My Wingtips*, AirLife Publishing, Shrewsbury, 2001, p.140. Flight Lieutenant Baveystock, DSO, DFC, DFM (1914–97), retired to farm in New Zealand after the war.

41 Internal memo, 4 April 1935, AIR 19/142, National Archives, London.

42 Sims, p.23.

43 AIR 19/142, National Archives, London.

44 Air Marshal P.B. Joubert to Air Marshal R.E.C. Peirse (Air Ministry), 13 July 1937, AIR 15/21, National Archives, London.

45 Undated, AIR 15/21, National Archives, London. My assumption about the date derives from the final quoted paragraph: Empire flying boats are in service with Imperial Airways, but Sunderlands are not yet with the RAF, which places the date at late 1937 or early 1938.

46 'Extracts from letter dated 29 October 1943 by CPT Lipscomb, Chief Engineer, Short Brothers, Rochester', Ms Papers 0419, folder 056, Alexander Turnbull Library, Wellington.

47 J.M. Preston, *A Short History: A History of Short Bros Aircraft Activities in Kent 1908–1964*, North Kent Books, Rochester, 1978.

48 Sir Arthur Gouge (1890–1962) was knighted in 1948. He became chief designer at Shorts in 1926 and from that date until 1943 was responsible for all aircraft design in the company. He was President of the Royal Aeronautical Society from 1942 to 1944. His recreations were horology and photography.

49 A. Gouge, 'Flying Boats and Their Possible Development', paper read in Newcastle on 8 March 1935 before the North East Coast Institution of Engineers and Shipbuilders, *Institution Transactions*, Volume 51, p.277.

50 Gouge, p.282.

51 Gouge, p.286.

52 'Secret' Report by L. Johnston, BSc, Report No BA 1286, March 1936, DSIR 23/5652, National Archives, London,

53 Kenneth Poolman, *Flying Boat*, William Kimber, London, 1962, p.17.

54 Sims, p.24. I have sighted a reference in the National Archives in London to a contract for a Short R.2/33 'Sunderland' prototype dated 16 October 1934 (No 351564/34); see AIR 2/2937. Gouge wrote to the Air Ministry on 1 November 1935 proposing a four-engined flying boat of about 60,000 pounds all-up weight to carry a downward-firing heavy gun for offensive action against ships and submarines. The proposal was summarily dismissed

and Gouge sternly advised to concentrate on serious matters; see AIR 2/1657.

55 Sims doubts this influence.

56 Gouge, p.287.

57 Sims, p.35.

58 *The Times*, 24 October 1962.

59 *The Times*, 15 March 1939.

60 The four-engined Lockheed Orion, currently in use as a long-range surveillance and anti-submarine aircraft, is perhaps the nearest modern, functionally equivalent aeroplane. As a 'shell', and without any electronic or weapons systems installed, an Orion cost about $NZ100 million in the 1990s.

61 *Coastal Command*, Crown Film Unit, 1942, COI 426, Imperial War Museum Film and Video Archive, London. The director was J.B. Holmes and the cameramen were Jonah Jones and Fred Gamage.

62 For some details of the crew who played parts, see John Evans, *Help from the Heavens: A History of No 228 Squadron, RAF*, Paterchurch Publications, Pembroke Dock, 1998, p.84. The Sunderland skipper in the film was played by Wing Commander 'Johnny' Hyde, formerly of 204 Squadron, who was killed in Beaufighter operations over Norway before the film premiered in London in October 1942.

63 Evison has been mentioned earlier. Gordon William Sutton was born in Auckland on 12 August 1913 and grew up in Ararimu in South Auckland.

64 The steamship *Blairlogie* (4425 tons) was sunk by U-30, commanded by Lieutenant Fritz-Julius Lemp, also responsible for the controversial torpedoing of the passenger ship *Athenia* on the first day of the war. Lemp sank seventeen ships in U-30 before being killed in the North Atlantic on 9 May 1941.

65 210 Squadron Operations Record Book, 17 September 1939, AIR 27/1298, National Archives, London. G.W. Sutton is buried in Pembroke Dock cemetery.

66 McGreal, pp.13–14.

67 AVIA 19/1014, National Archives, London.

68 FPRC Reports 285 and 292, AIR 57/5, National Archives, London.

69 F.C. Bartlett, FPRC Report 308, May 1941, AIR 57/5, National Archives, London.

70 Squadron Leader R.H. Winfield, 'Report on the Factors Influencing the Onset and Production of Fatigue in Catalina Flying Boat Crews', 18 August 1941, FPRC Report 355, AIR 57/5, National Archives, London.

71 AIR 27/1298, National Archives, London.

72 There are, of course, exceptions to the caution against open-sea alightings. Perhaps the most notable feat on record was Captain E.S. Alcock's forced alighting of the Imperial Airways Empire Boat *Cambria*, with no engines, on the high seas near Mozambique in March 1939. Alcock then 'sailed' the powerless *Cambria* into the safety of a bay. The story is told in Sims, pp.114–16. I notice from my father's post-war logbook that he was 'checked out' by Captain Alcock on Solent III G-AHIO in November 1951 before making the delivery flight of that aircraft for Trans Oceanic Airways from Southampton to Sydney.

73 Martin Gilbert, *The Churchill War Papers*, Volume III: 'The Ever-widening War 1941', William Heinemann, London, 2000, pp.21–22.

74   Gilbert, p.19.

75   Gilbert, p.184.

76   AIR 27/1414–1417, National Archives, London. Alec's logbook records the posting to 228 Squadron as taking effect from 6 December 1940.

77   Ernle Bradford, *Mediterranean: Portrait of a Sea*, Penguin Books, London, 1971, p.278.

78   The Acts of the Apostles, Chapter 27, verses 20 and 41–44 and Chapter 28, verses 1 and 2, as found in *The Bible: Authorized King James Version*, Oxford World's Classics, Oxford University Press, Oxford, 1998, pp. 186–88.

79   228 Squadron ORB, AIR 27/1414–1417, National Archives, London. Group Captain C.B.R. Pelly (later Air Marshal Pelly) was to become one of the key officers responsible for co-ordinating the evacuation from Greece.

80   Flight Lieutenant H.L.M. Glover was born in Dunedin, first joined the RAF in 1930, and flew for Imperial Airways until 1940, when he rejoined the RAF. He was the brother of the New Zealand poet Denis Glover.

81   228 Squadron ORB.

82   Peter Smith, who kindly explained to me that the 'eye-pennant' is the lower mooring attachment on the hull, told me in May 2003 that he had never heard of one of these solid structures being torn out before, and confirmed that the repair job would have been lengthy and difficult.

83   Viscount Cunningham of Hyndhope, *A Sailor's Odyssey*, Hutchinson, London, 1951, p.301.

84   Cunningham, p.303.

85   Later Air Marshal Sir Gilbert Nicholetts (1902–83). This distinguished flyer had considerable pre-war experience of long-distance flying and navigation. He took command of 228 Squadron in November 1938. He was later posted to the Far East and became a prisoner of war in 1942. After the war, he rose in 1956 to become Air Officer Commanding in Malta and Commander-in-Chief of Air Forces in the Mediterranean, and in 1958 Inspector-General of the RAF. His logbook is in the RAF Museum Library at Hendon (MF 10024/5).

86   Winston Churchill, *The Second World War*, Volume III, 'The Grand Alliance', Cassell, London, 1950, p.51.

87   Frederick Galea, *Call-Out*, Bieb Bieb, Malta, 2001. Duvauchelle and Melhouas were subsequently drafted into the RAF's 69 Squadron in Malta, flying Marylands, and were killed on 11 January 1941 when shot down near Catania in Sicily. I had the pleasure of meeting Frederick Galea at the excellent Aviation Museum at Ta'Qali in Malta in April 2005.

88   Muncheberg was born in Friedrichsdorf village, just north of Frankfurt, on 18 December 1918. After his Mediterranean period he went on to France, where he specialised in hunting Spitfires, and the Eastern Front. In 1942, he was sent to Tunisia where, on 23 March 1943, he was killed in an air battle with American Spitfires from the 52nd Fighter Group. Muncheberg was credited with the astonishing total of 135 aerial victories.

89   228 Squadron ORB, 10 March 1941.

90   For an indispensable account of the technical and strategic aspects, see F.H. Hinsley *et al*, *British Intelligence in the Second World War*, HMSO, London, 1979, Chapter 12.

91   It now appears clear that it was Dilly Knox's team in the 'cottage' at Bletchley Park which deciphered Admiral Iachino's signal about his operational plans

and provided the principal intelligence which guided Admiral Cunningham's force to the destruction of three Italian cruisers and two destroyers off Cape Matapan on 28 March 1941. See Mavis Batey's essay 'Breaking Italian Naval Enigma' in *Action This Day*, ed. Michael Smith and Ralph Erskine, Transworld Publishers, London, 2001, Chapter 6. Batey states that 'it was Dilly who rang the Admiralty immediately to make sure that when the battle was reported in the press its success should be accredited entirely to reconnaissance to cover the real source' (p.106).

92   The decision is dated 13 March 1941 and recorded in a note in 228 Squadron ORB.

93   Lawrence Durrell, *Clea*, Faber & Faber, London, 1960, pp.20–21.

94   Flying Accident Card (AM form 1180), 21 November 1940. Held at RAF Museum, Hendon.

95   Flying Accident Card (AM form 1180), 4 June 1941. Held at RAF Museum, Hendon.

96   Evelyn Waugh, *Officers and Gentlemen*, first published by Chapman & Hall, London, 1955; most accessible in *The Sword of Honour Trilogy*, Everyman's Library, London, 1994, p.350.

97   E.M. Forster, *Alexandria: A History and a Guide*, first published in Alexandria in 1922, first British edition with introduction by Lawrence Durrell, Haag, London, 1982, p.192.

98   Lawrence Durrell, introduction to Forster, p.x.

99   Report of Lieutenant Colonel Robert Lees, 22 February 1941, AIR 57/4, National Archives, London.

100 Durrell to Miller, 23 May 1944, in *The Durrell–Miller Letters 1935–1980*, ed. I.S. MacNiven, Faber & Faber, London, 1988, p.171.

101 Artemis Cooper, *Cairo in the War: 1939–1945*, Hamish Hamilton, London, 1989, pp.4–5.

102 In this Sunderland Alec had attacked and 'probably damaged' a submarine on 29 April 1942 when posted to Alexandria for a second period with 230 Squadron, from April to July 1942.

103 Bednall, pp.65–66.

104 Lord Byron, *Don Juan*, Canto III, verse 86(4), in *Lord Byron: The Complete Poetical Works*, ed. Jerome J. McGann, Volume V: *Don Juan*, Clarendon Press, Oxford, 1986, p.189.

105 Longmore, p.30.

106 Francis de Guignand, *Generals at War*, Hodder & Stoughton, London, 1964, p.37.

107 Anthony Eden, *The Eden Memoirs: The Reckoning*, Cassell, London, 1965, p.240.

108 Major-General R.J. Collins, *Lord Wavell (1883–1941): A Military Biography*, Hodder & Stoughton, London, 1948, p.372.

109 'The Campaign in Greece and Crete', *The Army at War*, issued for the War Office by the Ministry of Information, HMSO, London, 1942, p.13. The major part of this work, interesting as an official account at the time, was written by David Garnett (1892–1981), the novelist connected with the 'Bloomsbury Group'.

110 Freya Stark, *East Is West*, John Murray, London, 1945, p.98

111 General Sir Archibald Wavell, *Allenby: A Study in Greatness*, Oxford University Press, New York, 1941.

112 Wavell, p.295.

113 Collins, pp.340 and 381.

114 William Shakespeare, *The Tragedy of Anthony and Cleopatra*, ed. Michael Neill, Clarendon Press, Oxford, 1994, Act 1, Scene 2, line 184 (p.162).

115 Waugh, p.358.

116 Forster, p.33. The translation is by R.A. Furness.

117 Quoted in Poolman, p.93.

118 De Guignand, *Generals at War*, p.22. In an earlier work, *Operation Victory*, Hodder & Stoughton, 1947, de Guignand had presented a much more restrained analysis.

119 Sir John White, 'The Gamble of Greece: March-April 1941', unpublished typescript, generously provided to me by Sir John in 2002, p.1.

120 Meeting of Defence Committee (Operations) in Cabinet War Room, London, 8 January 1941, CAB 69/2, National Archives, London. Emphases added.

121 Paper by Chiefs of Staff Committee for the War Cabinet, 24 February 1941, CAB 66/15, National Archives, London, pp.68–71. The paper was signed by Dudley Pound, C. Portal, and R.H. Haining. Emphasis added.

122 Robin Higham, *Diary of a Disaster: British Aid to Greece 1940–1941*, University Press of Kentucky, Lexington, 1986, p.236.

123 Collins, pp.374 and 378.

124 John Connell, *Wavell: Scholar and Soldier*, Collins, London, 1964, p.414.

125 Longmore, p.275.

126 John Colville, *The Fringes of Power: Downing Street Diaries 1939–1945*, Hodder & Stoughton, London, 1985, p.373.

127 Gilbert, p.486.

128 Gilbert, p.488.

129 Gilbert, p.100.

130 Gilbert, p.514.

131 'B-G' has left a vivid account of these events in A. Heckstall-Smith and H.T. Baillie-Grohman, *Greek Tragedy '41*, Anthony Bland, London, 1961.

132 Diary of James William George Pickett, Ms Papers 4146, Alexander Turnbull Library, Wellington. Pickett, who was soon to be killed in Crete, had been an insurance agent in Auckland.

133 HMS *Kingston* and three other Royal Navy vessels took off 4720 New Zealand Division troops from Raphti, south-east of Athens, on 26 April. A further 4320 New Zealanders were evacuated from Monemvasia at the southern end of the Peloponnesus on the night of 28/29 April.

134 General Sir Iven Mackay (1882–1966) was the son of a Scots Presbyterian minister, and attended Sydney University before serving in World War I at Gallipoli, where he was wounded in the attack on Lone Pine. He later taught physics at the University of Sydney, and also served as High Commissioner for Australia in India. General Mackay's name, which appears accurately in Alec's logbook, has suffered corruption in the transfer to the 228 Squadron ORB and several subsequent histories, where it appears as 'General McCabe'. 230 Squadron ORB correctly states: 'A total of 39 passengers were loaded . . . Passengers included General Mackay and nine wounded'.

135 Quoted in Ivan D. Chapman, *Iven G Mackay: Citizen and Soldier*, Melway Publishing, Melbourne, 1975, p.232.

136 These events are also recorded in H.L. Thompson's *New Zealanders with the Royal Air Force*, Volume III, Government Printer, Wellington, 1959, p.40.

137 Chapman, p.232.

138 Heckstall-Smith and Baillie-Grohman, p.78.

139 Quoted in Gavin Long, *Greece, Crete and Syria*, Australian War Memorial and the Australian Government Publishing Service, Canberra, 1953, p.149.

140 Durrell to Miller, 13 March 1941, in MacNiven (ed.), p.147.

141 The entry for 25 April notes that 'the list of passengers carried is in No. 1001 file in the Adjutant's office', but this was apparently later lost in bombing at Malta.

142 Angelos Sikelianos (1884–1951). Quoted in Nikos Kazantzakis, *Journey to the Morea*, Simon & Schuster, New York, 1965, p.91.

143 Later Air Marshal Sir Rochford Hughes, OBE, AFC, DFC (Greek) (1914–96). Hughes was an Auckland-born journalist who had a distinguished war and post-war career with the RAF. For an account of his adventures when his Sunderland was shot down by two Me 110s near Benghazi in December 1941, see J.A. Whelan, *Malta Airmen*, War History Branch, Dept of Internal Affairs, Wellington, 1951, pp. 8–10.

144 'Squadron leader Hughes with the RAF', DAT 431 TK 28, Sound Archives, Radio New Zealand, Christchurch.

145 'The Campaign in Greece and Crete', p.43.

146 Air Vice-Marshal J.H. D'Albiac, 'Air Operations in Greece 1940–1941', supplement to *The London Gazette*, 7 January 1947.

147 Paul Freyberg, *Bernard Freyberg VC: Soldier of Two Nations*, Hodder & Stoughton, 1991, p.244.

148 Colville, p.443. Colville confesses surprise at Churchill's assertion that he had doubted the wisdom of the Greek venture: 'I seem to remember his influencing the decision in favour of an expedition and Dill being against it' (p.443).

149 General Freyberg's Order of the Day, 1 May 1941, Creforce Papers, WA 11/8/17 (Micro 3613), Archives New Zealand, Wellington.

150 Hansard, 7 May 1941, quoted in Gilbert, p.626.

151 From Harold Nicolson's Diary, quoted in Gilbert, p.630.

152 James Roosevelt (1907–91) had been secretary to his father in 1937–38 and is seen in photographs of the time almost literally holding up his father, who was crippled by polio. Jimmy went on active duty as a captain in the US Marine Corps in November 1940. Later in the war he was promoted to colonel and served with distinction in the Pacific theatre. After the war Jimmy went into politics for the Democrats and served from 1955 to 1965 as a congressman from California.

153 James Roosevelt and Sidney Shallett, *Affectionately, F.D.R. – A Son's Story of a Lonely Man*, Harcourt Brace, New York, 1959, p.330.

154 Joseph E. Persico, *Roosevelt's Secret War: FDR and World War II Espionage*, Random House, New York, 2001, p.104.

155 Roosevelt Press Conference No. 740 (2 May 1941), in *Complete Presidential Press Conferences of Franklin D. Roosevelt*, introduction by Jonathan Daniels, Da Capo Press, New York, 1972, Volume 17, pp.310–11

156 Chaz Bowyer, *The Short Sunderland*, Aston Publications, Bourne End, Buckinghamshire,1989, p.41. Wing Commander Geoffrey Francis, DFC, was awarded the DSO for his role in the evacuation of Greece, *The Times*, 21 July 1941.

157 Roosevelt and Shallett, p.332.

158 Jimmy's account has a front-line feel: 'Moving on to Iraq, we learned to hit the ditch and dive for foxholes to avoid enemy strafings. At the RAF's Air House one morning, Messerschmidts struck just as Major Thomas was

getting out of his pajamas, and he had to run for shelter in his birthday suit.'
Roosevelt and Shallett, p.332.

159 Churchill to Secretary of State for India, 10 April 1941, in Churchill, p.670.

160 Paraphrase of Telegram No 1470 dated 14 April 1941 from Averell Harriman
to FDR, 'Rush – Extreme Confidential for the President from Harriman'.
The paraphrase requirement was for security reasons. Franklin D. Roosevelt
Presidential Library and Museum, Digital Archives, File 338, www.fdrlibrary.
marist.edu/.

161 *New York Times*, 10 May, 1941.

162 James Roosevelt to Prime Minister Churchill, 16 June 1941, Churchill Papers,
CHAR/20/27/127–128, Churchill Archives Centre, Churchill College,
Cambridge. The Prime Minister's reply on 21 June via the American Embassy
in London was warm: 'Thank you so much for your letter. So sorry you could
not come this time. Am seeing Dickie Sunday' (CHAR/20/27/131).

163 Jimmy Roosevelt recorded that 'Our pilot, with admirable British nonchalance,
prepared us for a possible nighttime crack-up on the water by breaking out
a bottle of Scotch and saying: "Better have a nip – may be the last y'know".'
Quoted in Roosevelt and Shallett, p.333.

164 *Hansard*, 4 June 1940, 5th Series, Volume 361, columns 787–96.

165 Joseph P. Lash, *Roosevelt and Churchill 1939–1941*, Andre Deutsch,
London, 1977, p.426–27.

166 Lash, p.86.

167 Quoted in Robert E. Sherwood, *The White House Papers of Harry L.
Hopkins*, Eyre & Spottiswoode, London, 1948, Volume 1, p.129. Women
were considerably more 'isolationist' than men: 36 percent of women, and
only 29 percent of men agreed with the second and stronger position. The
isolationist leaders built on a certain retrospective resentment at American
losses in World War I.

168 Sherwood, p.130.

169 Lash, p.290.

170 Quoted in Lash, p.306

171 Stimson's diary, quoted in Lash, p.305. The role of Colonel Donovan is
examined below.

172 Lash, p.275.

173 Quoted in Sherwood, p.240.

174 Sherwood, p.256.

175 Sherwood, p.211.

176 Hinsley *et al.*, p.353.

177 Churchill, p.207.

178 The two decisions are set out and discussed in Hinsley *et al.*, pp.353 and
356.

179 Eden, p.190.

180 Eden, p.192. Havyatt was later killed in action.

181 Quoted in Lash, p.265. Lash states that 'The phrase had been coined by Jean
Monnet, who, after the collapse of France, had attached himself to the British
purchasing mission and who was being shepherded around Washington by
Justice Frankfurter. The latter heard him use it, and struck by its aptness,
immediately appropriated it for Roosevelt's use.'

182 Sherwood, p.224.

183 William Joseph ('Wild Bill') Donovan (1883–1959). President Eisenhower is
said to have exclaimed on hearing of Donovan's death in 1959: 'What a man!

We have lost the last hero.' For an account of Donovan's spectacular career, see Anthony Cave Brown, *The Last Hero: Wild Bill Donovan*, Times Books, New York, 1982.

184 Tony Simpson, *Operation Mercury: The Battle for Crete*, Hodder & Stoughton, London, 1981.

185 For an account of the difficulty and its solution, see Cave Brown, pp.151–52.

186 Thomas F. Troy, *Wild Bill and Intrepid: Donovan, Stephenson, and the Origins of the CIA*, Yale University Press, New Haven, 1996, p.78.

187 Brown, p.153.

188 Brown, p.155.

189 Dykes was killed returning from the Casablanca Conference in January 1943 when his Liberator transport crashed in Wales after engine failure.

190 Danchev, Alex, *Establishing the Anglo-American Alliance: The Second World War Diaries of Brigadier Vivian Dykes*, Brassey's, London, 1990, p.35, diary for Thursday, 16 January 1941.

191 The parenthetical speculation was Dykes's.

192 *Ambassador MacVeagh Reports*, ed. John O. Latrides, Princeton University Press, New Jersey, 1980, p.283.

193 Latrides (ed.), p.288.

194 Danchev, p.51.

195 Danchev, p.58, diary entry for 19 February 1941.

196 Bednall, p.65.

197 Eden, p.195.

198 Troy, pp.85–86.

199 Danchev, p.60, diary entry for 20 February 1941, emphases in original.

200 These views are reported by Anthony Eden in *The Eden Memoirs*, pp.197–8.

201 Danchev, p.54.

202 Danchev, p.61, diary entry for 24 February 1941.

203 228 Squadron ORB.

204 Telegram No 1295 to Viscount Halifax (Washington), 10 March 1941, 'personal and most secret . . . from Former Naval Person to the President', PREM 4/25/5, National Archives, London.

205 Eden to Churchill, 22 February 1941, PREM 4/25/5, National Archives, London. Churchill has minuted: 'we must vet his stuff first. He is good, but we must be very careful, having regard to operations'.

206 Eden to Churchill, Telegram No 361, 22 February 1941, PREM 4/25/5, National Archives, London.

207 Note by A. Bevir of 9 March 1941 and an explanation from a Government Hospitality Fund official of 10 March, PREM 4/25/5, National Archives, London.

208 Colville, p.361. Margesson was Secretary of State for War at the time.

209 Reported in Persico, p.91. The emphasis is added here.

210 Report by Colonel Donovan, PREM 4/25/5, National Archives, London.

211 Quoted in Lash, p.288.

212 FDR to Churchill, 11 April 1941, quoted in William L. Langer and S. Everett Gleason, *The Undeclared War 1940–1941*, Harper & Brothers, New York, 1953, p.435.

213 Langer and Gleason, p.434.

214 Churchill, p.540.

215 Quoted in Lash, p.490.

216 In addition to Flight Lieutenant Henry Lamond and Pilot Officer Bill Goldfinch, the survivors were Pilot Officer Sean Briscoe and Sergeant Davis. Those killed were Flying Officer J.C. Lylian, Pilot Officer J.H. Linton, Sergeant G. Cooper, Sergeant T. James, Sergeant R. Warren, and Leading Aircraftsman W. Sommers. See Evans, pp.28 and 87.

217 Henry Lamond to Alex Frame, 14 April 2003, letter in author's possession.

218 J.A. Whelan, *Malta Airmen*, War History Branch, Dept of Internal Affairs, Wellington, 1951, pp.7–8. Whelan, who himself served in flying boats with the RNZAF, was housemaster in Selwyn House at King's College in Auckland during my time as a boarder there from 1960 to 1963, and was one of my earliest teachers of history. It is another reminder of the modesty, approaching secrecy, of that generation of flying-boat men that, although I came to know and like John Whelan, this connection with my father's war experience was never mentioned to me by either man.

219 Whelan, p.8. See also H.L. Thompson, *New Zealanders with the Royal Air Force*, Volume III, Government Printer, Wellington, 1959, p.40.

220 Especially John Whelan's helpful chronicle of the events in *Malta Airmen*.

221 Lamond to the author, 14 April 2003. The reference to Alec's unlit night landing may relate to the occasion noted earlier when, on 12 January 1941, T9046 flew a 'special mission' to drop commandos in the Gulf of Hammamet off Tunisia.

222 Squadron-Leader H.W. Lamond to Wing Commander H.L. Thompson, RNZAF Historical Section, 24 March 1950, AIR 118/82(f), Archives New Zealand, Wellington.

223 W. Wynne Mason, *Prisoners of War*, War History Branch, Dept of Internal Affairs, Wellington, 1954, p.144.

224 Jack Hinton's account as told to Gabrielle McDonald may be found in her *Jack Hinton V.C.: A Man Amongst Men*, David Ling Publishing, Auckland, 1997, pp.77–87.

225 E.H. Simpson, 'Evacuation from Kalamata', Ms Papers 1479, Alexander Turnbull Library, Wellington. See also S.O. Playfair, 'The Mediterranean and Middle East', Volume II in J.R.M. Butler (ed.), *History of the Second World War*, HMSO, London, pp.102–3, where the circumstances of the surrender are discussed.

226 Sir John White, 'Crete', unpublished typescript provided to me by Sir John in 2001, p.9.

227 John Clement Julius Lylian was born in Ashburton, New Zealand, on 1 January 1920. In 1938 he travelled to England to attend the RAF College at Cranwell. After further training and conversion to flying boats at Calshot, he joined 228 Squadron at Pembroke Dock in March 1940 and went to the Mediterranean with the squadron in June that year, where he took part in the full range of operational flying. My father flew with him in the French Loire 130 on 17 February 1941. His body was not recovered after the crash of T9048 at Kalamata on 25 April 1941, and Flying Officer Lylian is regarded as 'lost at sea'. A death notice may be found in the *Otago Daily Times*, 14 May 1941.

228 An account of the mishap involving the Australian pilot (later Wing Commander) Vic Hodgkinson, DFC, on approach to Pembroke Dock on 28 April 1941 may be found in *Aeroplane*, August 2005, p.37. The writer there concludes that a false reading from the altimeter may have been responsible.

229 Henry Chancellor, *Colditz: The Definitive History*, Hodder & Stoughton, 2001, pp.334–35.

230 The ORB stated: '2/2/41. Squadron strengthened by arrival of 6 new pilots from No. 20 F.T.S. Rhodesia – P/O.s Goldfinch, Lovelace, Paré and Sergeants Burton, Massam and Davey'. All of these except Burton flew at one time or another with Alec. J.C. Paré later served alongside Alec in 230 Squadron, and under his command in 204 Squadron in 1944 when Paré was awarded the DFC on Alec's recommendation.

231 Peter Smith, *The Last Flying Boat: ML814 – Islander*, Ensign Publications, Southampton, 1993.

232 Diary of J.W.G. Pickett, Ms Papers 4146, Alexander Turnbull Library, Wellington.

233 'Major J.K. Elliott, Diary', MSX–4641, Alexander Turnbull Library, Wellington. Elliott (1908–1968) was at the time Deputy Assistant Director of Medical Services in Creforce and continued a distinguished military career to become a colonel.

234 'The Campaign in Crete – May 1940', AIR 41/29, Air Historical Branch (copy in the RAF Museum Library, Hendon), p.65.

235 Greetings to you great warriors of Aotearoa/New Zealand
    Both Maori and Pakeha – all, greetings.
    Although your bodies rest here in Crete,
    Your fame has returned home
    To your many marae in New Zealand.

236 Michael Davie (ed.), *The Diaries of Evelyn Waugh*, Weidenfeld & Nicolson, London, 1976, p.506. The spellings Imros and Imvros appear to be alternatives.

237 See PA Coll-1361 at the Alexander Turnbull Library, Wellington.

238 See Davie (ed.). From p.489 there appears a 20-page 'Memorandum on LAYFORCE; July 1940–July 1941', apparently written soon after Waugh's return from the Middle East, and describing his experience of the battle for Crete.

239 Davie (ed.), pp.506–7.

240 Davie (ed.), p.502.

241 Davie (ed.), p.507.

242 Davie (ed.), p.508.

243 Davie (ed.), p.509.

244 Waugh, p.448.

245 Geoffrey Cox, *A Tale of Two Battles*, William Kimber, London, 1987, p.105.

246 Waugh, p.450.

247 Both messages may be found in the Creforce papers, WA11/8/17 (Micro 3613), Archives New Zealand, Wellington.

248 This account relies on that provided in James Thorn, *Peter Fraser: New Zealand's Wartime Prime Minister*, Odhams Press, London, 1952, p.193.

249 *Oamaru Mail*, 31 May 1941.

250 Later Squadron Leader D.N. Milligan, DFC. Another New Zealander, Milligan was born in Wellington in 1916, joined the RAF in 1937, served in 238 and 230 Sunderland Squadrons, and was killed on a Beaufighter training flight in poor weather in January 1944.

251 Order No 138 of 30 May 1941, Appendices to 228 Squadron ORB, AIR 27/1417, National Archives, London.

252 Freyberg's batman, Private Hall, and his aide de camp, Lieutenant Jack Griffiths, a former All Black captain. Freyberg's personal assistant, Lieutenant J.C. White, had been sent off Crete by destroyer two days previously with important records.

253 Christopher Shores, *Air War for Yugoslavia, Greece & Crete*, Grub Street, London, 1987, p.397.

254 Keith Lindsay Stewart (1896–1972). See 'Brig Stewart', *Evening Post*, Wellington, 11 July 1946. Brigadier Stewart appears in the picture with General Freyberg in Fig.39.

255 Elliott, Diary. Elliott himself may have been aboard T9046. He is clearly on the Creforce list and may have been the 'Lt. Elliot' in the next footnote.

256 The passenger list for T9046 appears in the 228 Squadron ORB as follows: Brig. Brunskill, P/O James, Captain Purcell, Major Blythe, Lt. Comm. Mathias, Lt. Elliot, P/O Vernon, Marine Facer, Pte. Stewart, Major Latimer, Brigadier Stewart, Lt. Kemthorpe, Captain Mitchell, Major Hubert, Lt. Col. Maylor, LAC Deacon, Lt. Blackman, Captain Mothesdale, Major Clifford, Commander Thorp, Lt. Tsokolakis, Captain Flitton, Comm. Walkup, Pte. Edwards, Pte. Bradd. See AIR 27/1414–1417, National Archives, London.

257 Dan Davin, *Crete*, War History Branch, Dept of Internal Affairs, Wellington, 1953, p.438.

258 Recorded in Group Captain Beamish's subsequent 'Report on Air Operations in Crete', dated 11 June 1941 and compiled for General Freyberg. It may be found in the Creforce papers, WA 11/8/17 (Micro 3613), Archives New Zealand, Wellington.

259 Thorn, p.195.

260 The *Evening Post* on 2 June published a report from London dated 31 May that 'According to Berlin, the Cairo radio stated that General Freyberg was killed in a plane crash en route to Alexandria from Crete'.

261 *The Times*, 7 June 1941. Fraser also paid tribute to the risks run by the Royal Navy under Admiral Cunningham.

262 Colville, p.405 and p.403, footnote 1. By Fraser's departure in August 1941 Colville was much warmer: 'Mr Fraser, Prime Minister of New Zealand, who improves very much on acquaintance, came to say goodbye to the P.M. I showed him Dorothy Sayers' bitter poem about Ireland, which greatly took his fancy' (p.429). By 1944, Colville had learned to live with Fraser's lack of conversational sparkle: 'Mr Fraser told a number of boring stories about New Zealand at dinner, although he is really a nice enough old Scot with a good head on his shoulders' (p.487).

263 'Report by Flight Lieutenant A. Frame, No.228 Squadron, to Officer Commanding No.201 Group, RAF Middle East, 1 June 1941'. 228 Squadron ORB, Appendices. The 'other Sunderland' was 230 Squadron's N9029 – it picked up Major-General Weston and his staff. These were the last flights out of Crete.

264 *The Times*, 5 June 1941.

265 Davin, p.451.

266 *An Abridged History of the Greek–Italian and Greek–German War 1940–41*, Hellenic Army General Staff, Athens, 1997, p.284.

267 *London Gazette*, 11 July 1941, Volume III 1941, p.3995.

268 Quoted in Forster, p.63.

269 'Report of Pilot Officer L.G.M. Rees to Officer Commanding No. 201 Group, 8 June 1941', 228 Squadron ORB and Appendices.

270 Francis Bacon, *Essays*, introduced by Oliphant Smeaton, Dent, London, 1906, Essay V, 'Of Adversity', p.16.

271 General Sir Bernard Freyberg, VC, *Special Order of the Day*, Italy, 23 February 1945. Copy given to author by Sir John White.

272 Captain J.C. White, letter to family, 23 August 1942, copy given to the author by Sir John White in May 2002. As Freyberg's personal assistant, the young John White had been entrusted with a Leica camera and instructed to take photographs throughout the war. It is in this letter that White reported that 'the G. has presented me with all the negatives on condition that I have them available if and when they may be wanted by posterity or historians of the future'. The widespread use of Sir John's remarkable collection is testament to his loyal discharge of the general's instructions.

273 Stark, pp.129–30. Admiral Cunningham was present at the airfield also and gives the date as the 7th, rating Wavell as 'one of the great Generals thrown up by the war, if not the greatest' (*A Sailor's Odyssey*, p.402).

274 Gilbert, p.829.

275 Excerpt from John Mason's account, transcribed and provided by Neil Owen of Oban from the original in his possession with the explanation that 'John Mason was an old man of thirty when he wrote this. I understand he died in the early 60's from a heart attack.'

276 'Haboob ... a violent dust storm or sandstorm of northern Africa or India'. *Webster's Third New International Dictionary*, Merriam-Webster, Springfield, Massachusetts, 1993.

277 Excerpts from Carl van der Meulen's diary are quoted in Evans, p.31.

278 For details of the Eagle Rock crash, see Evans, pp.81–83.

279 The incident is recounted in Ken Delve's useful book, *Short Sunderland*, The Crowood Press, Marlborough, 2000, p.98.

280 Peter Fraser, remarks to a private meeting of the Empire Parliamentary Association, held at the House of Commons, Westminster, Tuesday, 12 July 1941, with the Rt. Hon. C.R. Attlee in the Chair, 'Papers Relating to 1941 Overseas Tour', McIntosh Papers, MS Papers 6759-012, Alexander Turnbull Library, Wellington. The text is corrected in Fraser's own hand.

281 Lord Gort, previously J.S.S.P. Vereker (1886–1946), won his VC in World War I. He commanded the expeditionary force in France in 1939 and directed the fall-back to and evacuation from Dunkirk. In 1941 he was Governor and Commander-in-Chief of Malta.

282 Admiral Sir James Somerville (1882–1949) commanded 'Force H' in the Western Mediterranean, responsible for maintaining shipping lines to Malta and the Middle East. His father had farmed sheep in New Zealand and his mother was from Tasmania.

283 Colville, p.435.

284 Richard Woodman, *Malta Convoys: 1940–1943*, John Murray, London, 2000, pp.217–18.

285 C. Shores and Brian Cull, with Nicola Malizia, *Malta: The Spitfire Year 1942*, Grub Street, London, 1991, p.90.

286 'Informal diary', 490 Squadron (NZ), AIR 173/2, Archives New Zealand, Wellington. Photographs of Fifth Avenue and Yankee Stadium, pasted into the diary, attest to the enthusiasm of the tourists.

287 'Informal diary', 490 Squadron (NZ), AIR 173/1, Archives New Zealand, Wellington. Ten years later, the party was resumed from time to time in Tahiti when Joe Shephard, and other wartime comrades, would meet Alec

for a beer at the Cercle Polynésien on the Papeete waterfront at the end of
TEAL's Coral Route.

288 The sole survivor was Flying Officer F.A. Brittain, who was seriously injured.
Bill Dodds was the son of Mr and Mrs J.S. Dodds of 9 Trent Street, Oamaru.
He attended Waitaki Boys' High School in the period 1933–35.

289 *Hansard*, 4 June 1940, 5th Series, Volume 361, columns 787–96.

290 'Major J.K. Elliott, Diary', MSX–4641, Alexander Turnbull Library,
Wellington.

291 Churchill to Longmore, 29 March 1941, quoted in 'The Campaign in Crete
– May 1940', p.127.

292 Quoted in Gilbert, pp.250–51.

293 Longmore, p.282.

294 Longmore, p.286.

295 Air Officer Commanding in Chief Tedder, 3/6/41, quoted in 'The Campaign
in Crete – May 1941', p.71.

List of Abbreviations

a/c	aircraft
BOAC	British Overseas Airways Corporation
CIA	Central Intelligence Agency
CIGS	Chief of Imperial General Staff
COI	Co-ordinator of Intelligence
DFC	Distinguished Flying Cross
FDR	Franklin Delano Roosevelt
GMT	Greenwich Mean Time
MLC	mechanised landing craft
ORB	Operations Record Book
OSS	Office of Special Operations
PD or 'Pee Dee'	Pembroke Docks
RAF	Royal Air Force
RAI	Réseau Aérien Interinsulaire
RNZAF	Royal New Zealand Air Force
S.O.S.	secours au secours (distress call)
T.O.	take-off
TEAL	Tasman Empire Airways Limited
VC	Victoria Cross
WAAF	Women's Auxiliary Air Force

Bibliography

1. Books and Journal Articles

Bacon, Sir Francis, *Essays*, introduced by Oliphant Smeaton, Dent, London, 1906

Batey, Mavis, 'Breaking Italian Naval Enigma', Chapter 6 in *Action This Day*, ed. Michael Smith and Ralph Erskine, Transworld Publishers, London, 2001

Baveystock, Leslie, *Wavetops at My Wingtips*, AirLife Publishing, Shrewsbury, 2001

Bednall, Dundas, *Sun on My Wings*, Paterchurch Publications, Pembroke Dock, 1989

Bowyer, Chaz, *Short Sunderland*, Aston Publications, Bourne End, Buckinghamshire, 1989

Bradford, Ernle, *Mediterranean: Portrait of a Sea*, Penguin Books, London, 1971

Byron, Lord, *The Complete Poetical Works*, ed. Jerome J. McGann, Volume V: *Don Juan*, Clarendon Press, Oxford, 1986

Cate, Curtis, *Antoine de Saint-Exupéry: His Life and Times*, Heinemann, London, 1970

Cave Brown, Anthony, *The Last Hero: Wild Bill Donovan*, Times Books, New York, 1982

Chancellor, Henry, *Colditz: The Definitive History*, Hodder & Stoughton, London, 2001

Chapman, Ivan D., *Iven G Mackay: Citizen and Soldier*, Melway Publishing, Melbourne, 1975

Churchill, Winston S., *The Second World War*: Volume III, 'The Grand Alliance', Cassell & Co, London, 1950

Collins, Major-General R.J., *Lord Wavell (1883–1941): A Military Biography*, Hodder & Stoughton, London, 1948

Colville, John, *The Fringes of Power: Downing Street Diaries 1939–1945*, Hodder & Stoughton, London, 1985

Complete Presidential Press Conferences of Franklin D. Roosevelt, introduced by Jonathan Daniels, Da Capo Press, New York, 1972, Volume 17

Connell, John, *Wavell: Scholar and Soldier*, Collins, London, 1964

Cooper, Artemis, *Cairo in the War: 1939–1945*, Hamish Hamilton, London, 1989

Cox, Geoffrey, *A Tale of Two Battles*, William Kimber, London, 1987

Cunningham, Viscount, of Hyndhope, *A Sailor's Odyssey*, Hutchinson, London, 1951

Danchev, Alex, *Establishing the Anglo-American Alliance: The Second World War Diaries of Brigadier Vivian Dykes*, Brassey's, London, 1990

Davie, Michael (ed.), *The Diaries of Evelyn Waugh*, Weidenfeld & Nicolson, London, 1976

Davin, Dan, *Crete*, War History Branch, Dept of Internal Affairs, Wellington, 1953

de Guignand, F., *Generals at War*, Hodder & Stoughton, London, 1964

de Guignand, F., *Operation Victory*, Hodder & Stoughton, London, 1947

Delve, Ken, *Short Sunderland*, The Crowood Press, Marlborough, 2000

Durrell, Lawrence, *Clea*, Faber & Faber, London, 1960

Duval, G.R, *British Flying-Boats and Amphibians 1909–1952*, Putnam, London, 1966

Eden, Anthony, *The Eden Memoirs: The Reckoning*, Cassell, London, 1965

Evans, John, *Help from the Heavens: A History of No. 228 Squadron, RAF*, Paterchurch Publications, Pembroke Dock, 1998

Forster, E.M., *Alexandria: A History and a Guide*, first published in Alexandria in 1922, first British edition with introduction by Lawrence Durrell, Haag, London, 1982

Frame, Janet, *To the Is-land*, The Women's Press, Auckland, 1983

Freyberg, Paul, *Bernard Freyberg VC: Soldier of Two Nations*, Hodder & Stoughton, London, 1991

Galea, Frederick, *Call-Out*, Bieb Bieb, Malta, 2001

Garnett, David, 'The Campaign in Greece and Crete', in *The Army at War*, issued for the War Office by the Ministry of Information, HMSO, London, 1942

Gilbert, Martin, *The Churchill War Papers*, Volume III: 'The Ever-widening War 1941', Heinemann, London, 2000

Gouge, Arthur, 'Flying Boats and Their Possible Development', paper read in Newcastle on 8 March 1935 before the North East Coast Institution of Engineers and Shipbuilders, *Institution Transactions*, Volume 51, p.277

Heckstall-Smith, A. and Baillie-Grohman, H.T., *Greek Tragedy '41*, Anthony Bland, London, 1961

Hellenic Army General Staff, *An Abridged History of the Greek–Italian and Greek–German War 1940–41*, Athens, 1997

Higham, Robin, *Diary of a Disaster: British Aid to Greece 1940–1941*, University Press of Kentucky, Lexington, 1986

Hinsley, F.H. *et al.*, *British Intelligence in the Second World War*, HMSO, London, 1979

Homer, *The Odyssey*, translated by Edward McCrorie, with introduction by Richard P. Martin, Johns Hopkins University Press, Baltimore, 2004

Hoston, Fred W. and Matthew E. Rodina Jr, *Grumman Mallard: The Enduring Classic*, Robin Brass Studio, Montreal, 2006

Kazantzakis, Nikos, *Journey to the Morea*, Simon & Schuster, New York, 1965

Langer, William L. and S. Everett Gleason, *The Undeclared War 1940–1941*, Harper & Brothers, New York, 1953

Lash, Joseph P., *Roosevelt and Churchill 1939 –1941*, Andre Deutsch, London, 1977

Latrides, John O. (ed.), *Ambassador MacVeagh Reports: Greece 1933–1947*, Princeton University Press, Princeton, New Jersey, 1980

Long, Gavin, *Greece, Crete and Syria,* Australian War Memorial and the Australian Government Publishing Service, Canberra, 1953

Longmore, Sir Arthur, *From Sea to Sky*, Geoffrey Bles, London, 1946

MacNiven, I.S. (ed.), *The Durrell–Miller Letters 1935–1980*, Faber & Faber, London, 1988

McDonald, Gabrielle, *Jack Hinton V.C.: A Man Amongst Men*, David Ling Publishing, Auckland, 1997

McGreal, Maurice, *A Noble Chance: One Pilot's Life*, McGreal, Wellington, 1994

McLean, Gavin, *Oamaru Harbour: Port in a Storm*, Dunmore Press, Palmerston North, 1982

McNeish, James, *Dance of the Peacocks*, Vintage, Auckland, 2003

Martyn, Errol W., *For Your Tomorrow*, Volplane Press, Christchurch, 1998 (two volumes)

Mason, W. Wynne, *Prisoners of War*, War History Branch, Dept of Internal Affairs, Wellington, 1954

Mulgan, John, *Report on Experience*, Blackwood & Janet Paul, Auckland, 1967. First published by Oxford University Press, 1947

Nicolson, Harold, *Diaries and Letters 1939–45*, Collins, London, 1967

Oamaru Borough Council, *Municipal History of Oamaru*, Oamaru, 1936

Ovenden, Keith, *A Fighting Withdrawal*, Oxford University Press, Oxford, 1996

Persico, Joseph E., *Roosevelt's Secret War: FDR and World War II Espionage*, Random House, New York, 2001

Playfair, S.O., 'The Mediterranean and Middle East', Volume II in J.R.M. Butler (ed.), *History of the Second World War*, HMSO, London

Poolman, Kenneth, *Flying Boat*, William Kimber, London, 1962

Preston, J.M., *A Short History: A History of Short Bros Aircraft Activities in Kent 1908–1964*, North Kent Books, Rochester, 1978

Roosevelt, James and Sidney Shallett, *Affectionately, F.D.R. – A Son's Story of a Lonely Man*, Harcourt Brace, New York, 1959

Saint-Exupéry, Antoine de, *Terre des Hommes*, Heinemann, London, 1951

Shakespeare, William, *The Tragedy of Anthony and Cleopatra*, ed. Michael Neill, Clarendon Press, Oxford, 1994

Sherwood, Robert E., *The White House Papers of Harry L. Hopkins*, Eyre & Spottiswoode, London, 1948

Shores, Christopher, *Air War for Yugoslavia, Greece & Crete: 1940–41*, Grub Street, London, 1987

Shores, Christopher, and Brian Cull, with Nicola Malizia, *Malta: The Spitfire Year 1942*, Grub Street, London, 1991

Simpson, Tony, *Operation Mercury: The Battle for Crete*, Hodder & Stoughton, London, 1981

Sims, Phillip E., *Adventurous Empires*, AirLife Publishing, Shrewsbury, 2000

Smith, E.H., 'Guns Against Tanks', *New Zealand in the Second World War*, War History Branch, Dept of Internal Affairs, Wellington, 1948

Smith, Peter, *The Last Flying Boat: ML814 – Islander*, Ensign Publications, Southampton, 1993

Stark, Freya, *East Is West*, John Murray, London, 1945

Thompson, H.L., *New Zealanders with the Royal Air Force*, Government Printer, Wellington, 1959 (three volumes)

Thorn, James, *Peter Fraser: New Zealand's Wartime Prime Minister*, Odhams Press, London, 1952

Troy, Thomas F., *Wild Bill and Intrepid: Donovan, Stephenson, and the Origins of the CIA*, Yale University Press, New Haven, 1996

Waugh, Evelyn, *Officers and Gentlemen*, Chapman & Hall, London, 1955; with Introduction by Frank Kermode, Everyman's Library, London, 1994

Wavell, General Sir Archibald, *Allenby: A Study in Greatness*, Oxford University Press, New York, 1941

Whelan, J.A., *Malta Airmen*, War History Branch, Dept of Internal Affairs, Wellington, 1951

Woodman, Richard, *Malta Convoys: 1940–1943*, John Murray, London, 2000

2. Archival and Other Sources

210 Squadron (RAF), Operations Record Book, AIR 27/1298, National Archives, London

228 Squadron (RAF), Operations Record Book and Appendices, AIR 27/1414–1417, National Archives, London

230 Squadron (RAF), Operations Record Book, AIR 27/1422, National Archives, London

490 Squadron, informal diary, AIR 173/2, Archives New Zealand, Wellington

Beamish, Group Captain, 'Report on Air Operations in Crete', dated 11 June 1941 and compiled for General Freyberg, Creforce Papers, Micro 3613 (WA 11/8/17), Archives New Zealand, Wellington

Bolland, G.A., 'A Guy from Coastal Command: the Autobiography of Group Captain G.A. Bolland, CBE', typescript with photographs, accession no X003-1877, Royal Air Force Museum Library, Hendon, London

'The Campaign in Greece 1940–1941', AIR 41/28, Air Historical Branch (copy in Royal Air Force Museum Library, Hendon, London)

'The Campaign in Crete – May 1940', AIR 41/29, Air Historical Branch (copy in Royal Air Force Museum Library, Hendon, London)

Churchill Papers, CHAR/20/27/127–128, Churchill Archives Centre, Churchill College, Cambridge

Coastal Command, Crown Film Unit, 1942, COI 426, Imperial War Museum Film and Video Archive, London

Creforce Papers, Micro 3613 (WA 11/8/17), Archives New Zealand, Wellington

D'Albiac, Air Vice-Marshal J.H., 'Air Operations in Greece 1940–1941', Supplement to *The London Gazette*, 7 January 1947

Elliott, J.K., Diary, MSX–4641, Alexander Turnbull Library, Wellington

Johnstone, L., 'Secret' Report No B.A. 1286, March 1936, DSIR 23/5652, National Archives, London

'Methods of Entry into the RAF by New Zealanders 1919-1938', AIR 118/56, Archives New Zealand, Wellington

Milner Frank, 'Diary of Trip', Ms Papers 0051–064, Alexander Turnbull Library, Wellington

Notes on New Zealand applicants for Short-Service Commissions in RAF, AIR 118/76 (a)–(f), Archives New Zealand, Wellington

Pickett, James William George, Diary, Ms Papers 4146, Alexander Turnbull Library, Wellington

Report by Colonel Donovan, PREM 4/25/5, National Archives, London

Simpson, E.H., 'Evacuation from Kalamata', Ms Papers 1479, Alexander Turnbull Library, Wellington

'Squadron leader Hughes with the RAF', DAT 431 TK 28, Sound Archives, Radio New Zealand, Christchurch

White, Sir John, 'Crete', unpublished typescript provided to author by Sir John in 2001

White, Sir John, 'The Gamble of Greece: March-April 1941', unpublished typescript provided to author by Sir John in 2001

Winfield, Squadron Leader R.H., 'Report on the Factors Influencing the Onset and Production of Fatigue in Catalina Flying Boat Crews', 18 August 1941, FPRC Report 355, AIR 57/5, National Archives, London.

Acknowledgements

My previous books and articles have been about law and lawyers. This project came closer to home and made me turn for help towards family and my father's wartime comrades and friends. I must first thank my father's comrades, Henry Lamond, Bill Goldfinch, and Eric Harrison in England, and Maurice McGreal in New Zealand, who warmly gave their time and wisdom to my neophyte questions about the times and conditions they shared with my father. Sir John White, present at Freyberg's side in the events of 1941, was a generous and wise guide to 1941 Middle East events from the New Zealand Division point of view, and Lady White made me feel welcome in her home for several long discussions. My close family have been very supportive. My sisters, Susan Glenn and Margaret Bunce, and my cousin Tim Williamson and his wife Lorraine, have responded to questions, found photographs, and contributed memories and interpretations which have added to the reconstruction attempted here. Our cousin Sandy MacDonald has helped my understanding of family matters also. Extended family must be thanked too. Karl and Natalie Urban provided both work-space and encouragement in Vancouver as the structure first emerged in August 2003. I also thank some friends for their encouragement, inspiration, and help of many kinds over a long period. Max McDonnell, musician of Rotorua; Mark Wilson in Melbourne; Tim Brosnahan in Wellington who read a draft encouragingly; Mike Mitchell, of Rarotonga, who indirectly helped decide the title and gave usefully honest advice on an early draft; Peter Walker and long lunches in Wellington and London; Harry Ricketts, poet and critic in Wellington, who helped me to believe that a flying boat might be the centre-point of the story; and Paul Meredith, who tolerated my deviations from our collaboration on customary law. As I travelled for the book, debts were accumulated. John Evans' help at Pembroke Dock is recorded in the text. Paul Walker and Jo Andrews were warm-hearted hosts in London. Kathleen and Tony Bradley revived a weary researcher with lunch and talk amid bluebells in Oxford. Manousos in Crete, and Omar and Mando in Alexandria appear in photographs. Frederick Galea was most helpful in Malta. Neil Owen generously shared his extensive knowledge of Sunderland squadrons in Oban in 1941. Libraries, and the patience and professionalism of their staff, were important to the project. I should mention in particular the Royal New Zealand Air Force Museum at Wigram, who proved to be worthy custodians of my father's wartime logbook, and who do a great job with limited resources. The Imperial War Museum in London, and particularly its excellent photographic archive. The National Archives at Kew, near London, efficient and comprehensive as ever, were an indispensable source. In Wellington, the National Library and Archives New Zealand provided help. Fergus Barrowman and his team at Victoria University Press managed as on previous occasions to blend a friendly approach with high professional standards, and I must particularly record my debt to the fine editorial work of Andrew Mason on the early manuscript. As always, my partner Lorraine Williams has been a vital support in the research and writing, for which she is lovingly thanked.

Index